Praise for *The Socially Networked Classroom: Teaching in the New Media Age*

"Kist chronicles his journey in both the classroom and online, as well as that of many other teachers navigating these new spaces with their students. He writes as a learner should, sharing what he discovers along the way. I appreciate the notes from the road, and I suspect educators will find much to take back to their classrooms. I especially like that he asks important questions while capturing how he and several other master teachers have attempted to ask and answer them with their own students. You will, too."

Bud Hunt
http://budtheteacher.com
Instructional Technologist
St. Vrain Valley School District
Longmont, Colorado

"The innovative classroom activities in this engaging book will inspire teachers to help students acquire digital-media literacies for collaborating on and sharing their work—literacies essential for participation in a networked world."

Richard Beach
Professor of English Education
University of Minnesota

"This book marks our place in the whirlwind transformation of Internet technology that launched users, in a surprisingly sudden (and often unnoticed) leap, from Web 1.0 to Web 2.0. Kist shows educators both a mirror and a map, explaining where we are and where we might go in this vastly rich frontier of knowledge and learning. The paths he shows us spill into layered networks of interconnections and intersections—a true 'web' of knowledge—replacing old, tired, and narrow paths."

Sharon Elin, NBCT
Instructional Technology Integrator
Chesterfield County Public Schools
Chesterfield, Virginia

"A veritable smorgasbord of ideas and suggestions. This text grabbed me right away, and I started flagging all sorts of ideas even in the earliest chapters. It is as if Bill Kist met me in the hallway, took me by the hand, and simply said, 'Come here, I want to show you something.'"

Sheila M. Gragg, MEd
Technology Integration Coach
Ashbury College
Ottawa, Ontario

"I loved this book. I learned a great deal about 'texts' and about how to teach them to students in the digital age. But what was so compelling about this book was the genuineness of the author; he cares passionately about his students and passionately about the subject matter. As Dewey points out, effective education must have an emotional component; indeed, the book's credibility and authority are derived from its core emotional energy."

Elliot Soloway, Arthur F. Thurnau Professor
Dept. of EECS, College of Engineering
University of Michigan
Ann Arbor, Michigan

"This book is totally compelling and geared to a slice of the teaching profession that is in desperate need of the kind of guidance and insight Kist offers. By sharing his creative teaching methods, he points out the openings in teachers' practice where shift can happen."

Sue Collins
Integration Technology Specialist
Bedford Public Schools
Bedford, Massachusetts

The Socially Networked Classroom

Teaching in the NEW MEDIA AGE

William Kist

Foreword by
Kylene Beers

For information:

Corwin
A SAGE Company
2455 Teller Road
Thousand Oaks, California 91320
(800) 233-9936
Fax: (800) 417-2466
www.corwinpress.com

SAGE Ltd.
1 Oliver's Yard
55 City Road
London EC1Y 1SP
United Kingdom

SAGE India Pvt. Ltd.
B 1/I 1 Mohan Cooperative
Industrial Area
Mathura Road, New Delhi 110 044
India

SAGE Asia-Pacific Pte. Ltd.
33 Pekin Street #02-01
Far East Square
Singapore 048763

Printed in the United States of America

Library of Congress Cataloging-in-Publication Data

Kist, William.
The socially networked classroom: teaching in the new media age/William Kist; foreword by Kylene Beers.
p. cm.
Includes bibliographical references and index.
ISBN 978-1-4129-6700-6 (cloth)
ISBN 978-1-4129-6701-3 (pbk.)
1. Internet in education. 2. Online social networks. I. Title.

LB1044.87.K58 2010
371.33'46754—dc22 2009025295

This book is printed on acid-free paper.

09 10 11 12 13 10 9 8 7 6 5 4 3 2 1

Acquisitions Editor: Carol Chambers Collins
Editorial Assistant: Brett Ory
Production Editor: Jane Haenel
Copy Editor: Jeannette McCoy
Typesetter: C&M Digitals (P) Ltd.
Proofreader: Theresa Kay
Indexer: Sheila Bodell
Cover and Graphic Designer: Karine Hovsepian

Contents

Foreword

Preparing Students for a World Gone Flat

One year and seven months ago, I was asked a question by a high school principal. I couldn't answer his question then. Now, finally, I can.

* * *

I'm often in schools, mostly middle schools and high schools, and while there I find the opportunity to have some one-on-one time with the principal. When that happens, I will invariably ask him or her my favorite question: "What type of student will *not* do well in this school?"

I like the question because it always catches principals by surprise, something that's generally hard to do. They expect the what-type-of-student-*will*-do-well question and have that answer down pat: "Students who are willing to work hard in the classroom and participate in any of our many extracurricular activities and be good citizens will do fine. . . ." But to consider who *won't* be successful in the school, one must see the school from another point of view. One very honest principal in a large urban high school took his time with this question and finally answered, "Now that you have me thinking about it, I don't think this school would be good for a student who needs big blocks of time to process information." I asked why, and he explained, "We're still working off a factory model of education, moving kids quickly from one class to the next every 42 minutes with no processing time between classes just so we can get them in and out of seven classes during the day. I think that could be a hard way to learn for some kids."

We both sat quietly in his small office, looking out the window to the school's athletic field where kids were running laps. After a moment, he continued, "Is there even any research that says that 42 minutes is enough to learn anything meaningful?" We talked about the lack of research that supports why a class period is any particular length of time and then sat thinking about the things we do in schools that don't make much sense. Eventually, he added, "Actually, it's not just that we run this school by a bell system—something straight from the factory whistle that ushered workers back to work after breaks—but that our entire model for education comes from the industrial age. During that time, making sure each person on the assembly line could handle discreet skills was important. That's what we're doing here today in this school—making sure these kids can all handle discreet skills. I'm not sure we ever try to give them the big picture or, more important, get them to create the big picture themselves. We're teaching kids to pass a test, but I don't think we're making sure they can be competitive in the world they'll live in for the next 40, 50 years." He paused, but before I could respond, he jumped back in: "Let me answer your question again. Who won't do well in this school? Anyone wanting an education that is truly preparation for this flat world."[1]

* * *

This principal was far more honest than most and probably offered too strong an indictment of his school. But, as our conversation continued, it became apparent that the students were attending a school that looked much like the school the principal attended some 35 years ago when he was in high school. Desks were still, more often than not, in rows. Metal file cabinets still sat by classroom doors. And while chalk had been replaced with erasable markers and blackboards had become white boards, teachers still used the wall as the primary teaching tool. Collaboration was still about talking with the person behind you, and publishing work was about hanging it in the hallway. Sure, in this high school there were computers in every classroom, but they were mainly used for word processing or for viewing a Web site the teacher had found. The overhead projector was now an LCD projector, and the mimeographed worksheet had given way to the photocopied worksheet, while transparencies had been put aside for PowerPoint presentations. But those changes had not affected the "show-and-tell philosophy" (to borrow the principal's words) of most of the teachers: "The teachers show the kids what they want them to know, and the kids tell it back to them on the test."

In this school, smart phones and iPods were off limits; few teachers encouraged students to blog; fewer used classroom wikis as a way to work collaboratively; and none were using tools such as Google Docs, Twitter, Diigo, or Del.icio.us. The principal concluded, "We're creating another generation of students who know how to consume information, when what we need to be nurturing is a generation that knows how to produce new ideas." Then he asked me a question: "I've got a little money. What

---

[1] He's referring to Thomas Friedman's *The World Is Flat* (Farrar, Straus and Giroux, 2005).

book would you suggest I buy for my faculty so that we can all learn how to better prepare our students for this flat world?"

I thought of some titles, but none of them were just right. None of the books painted a rich enough description of how to transform a classroom into a 21st-century room. None of them offered the details needed to provide the confidence one needs when attempting new instructional strategies that use new tech tools. None of them blended old technologies (paper and pen) with new technologies (blogs and wikis), with assessment rubrics I could use tomorrow. None of them allowed each of us to be at a different place on the continuum of learning as we entered the book. None of them did that because none of them were *this* book.

* * *

This book asks us if the social interactivity of the Web—Web 2.0—has "transformed the way we 'do' school," and then shows us, with care and specificity, the way to transform our schools. If you're a novice, you'll want to start with the "Short" and "Tall" chapters (think Starbucks coffee). If you've been thinking about new literacies for a while, then you can head to the "Grande" chapter. If you're thinking about writing your own book, then you'll turn to the "Venti" chapter. No matter the chapter, you'll find excellent ideas. As Bill points out, the coffee in Starbucks is the same whether the cup size is small or large. The difference is the amount. That's the difference you'll find in the various chapters. If you're only beginning to think about social networking in your classroom, the suggestions in the "Short" chapter will be perfect for you.

Regardless of the chapter, Bill asks us to consider what happens when our classrooms become as big as the world. I would change the question a bit to echo the question I asked the principal: "What happens when our classrooms *do not* become as big as the world?" I suggest that one result might be a diminished educational experience that in all likelihood prepares students to pass state-mandated tests but probably doesn't prepare them for living in a global economy, for living in a world gone flat. We need to transform the way we do school because the digitalization of information and automation of jobs has transformed the way we socialize and work. All too often I hear administrators, teachers, or parents say that kids just need the basics; or worse, I hear them say that underachieving students need the basics. When I asked one principal to define "basics," he said, "You know. Reading and writing. Good solid basics." I reminded him that at one time in this country a basic level of literacy was the ability to sign one's name. "*That* basic?" I asked. He said that was ridiculous because, "of course, what is now basic has changed."

And that's the point. What's *basic* has changed. Change is rarely easy. If you are old enough to sing the first few lines of "Tie a Yellow Ribbon Round an Old Oak Tree," then you'll remember using the big film projectors in a classroom. (And if you aren't old enough to sing along, then you understand immediately the importance of prior knowledge.) The film would break, and we would hope for a 14-year-old in the classroom who could splice it and get the film started again. None of us would embrace that technology today, yet many of us wondered about bringing VCRs and then DVDs into the classroom when that technology emerged. And now, we wonder again with YouTube and streaming news. We hesitate to go forward, and yet, once there, we would not go backward.

Early in this book, Bill tells us that, as he considered his own teaching, he realized that "not only did I need to 'walk the walk,' I needed to pick up the pace." Picking up the pace will mean different things for different readers, and Bill recognizes that. So, no matter where you are on your own journey of creating a "socially networked classroom," you'll find the chapter that fits your needs. Each chapter is filled with rich descriptions, detailed explanations of activities, and rubrics that help us assess student work. More than that, though, each chapter offers us a glimpse of what it could mean to create a classroom as big as the world. That's the real reason this book is the answer to the principal's question. I suspect you'll find it answers many of your questions, too.

Kylene Beers, EdD
Senior Reading Advisor to Secondary Schools
Reading and Writing Project
Teachers College
Author of When Kids Can't Read/What Teachers Can Do

Acknowledgments

This book would not exist without the encouragement of Carol Chambers Collins, acquisitions editor for Corwin. Carol edited my first book at Teachers College Press, and when we met at the National Council of Teachers of English Annual Convention in November of 2007 in New York, she suggested I might want to do another book, this time focusing on social networking in classrooms. I was hesitant because I was working on some other projects at the time and moving through a change in the courses I was teaching, but with the encouragement of my wife, Stephanie, I decided to take Carol's suggestion and start exploring the writing of another book. I'm so glad I did because this decision sent me down a path not only of learning about teachers who are using Web 2.0 in their classrooms but also of reconsidering my own teaching in light of what I was learning. Carol has not only made my copy read better, but she has also informed my scholarship.

In examining this book and all of the different projects and activities I've done over the years, I've realized more than ever the debt I owe to my current and former students—high school students and both preservice and inservice teachers with whom I've worked. Their willingness to plunge in and give these ideas a chance has helped refine and enrich my work.

Finally, I have to acknowledge the teachers I have profiled in this book and who have formed the major subject of most of my earlier writings as well. Their courage inspires me and, I feel, will be viewed decades from now as forming the foundation of a new way of doing school.

Links for Some Educators Profiled in This Book

Paul Allison
http://youthvoices.net/home

Frank Baker
Blog: http://ncte-ama.blogspot.com
www.frankwbaker.com

Mollie Blackburn
Kaleidoscope Youth Center
www.kycohio.org

Elizabeth A. Boeser
missboeser.googlepages
.com

William Chamberlain
www.noeltigers.com

Tom Daccord
http://edtechteacher.org

Clarence Fisher
http://remoteaccess.typepad.com

Elizabeth Helfant
http://helcat.org/wordpress

Renee Hobbs
www.mediaeducationlab.com

Tom Liam Lynch
www.tomliamlynch.org

Angela Maiers
www.angelamaiers.com

George Mayo
www.mrmayo.org

Erin Reilly
www.zoeysroom.com

Mike Slowinski
www.c3po.us

Kimberly Whitaker
http://ehsfreerice.pbwiki.com

Publisher's Acknowledgments

Corwin gratefully acknowledges the contributions of the following reviewers:

Sue Collins, Integration Technology Specialist, Bedford Public Schools, Bedford, Massachusetts

Sharon Elin, NBCT, Instructional Technology Integrator, Chesterfield County Public Schools, Chesterfield, Virginia

Sheila M. Gragg, MEd, Technology Integration Coach, Ashbury College, Ottawa, Ontario

Sandra Moore, High School English Teacher, Coupeville High School, Coupeville, Washington

Elliot Soloway, Arthur F. Thurnau Professor, Dept. of EECS, College of Engineering, University of Michigan, Ann Arbor, Michigan

About the Author

William Kist is an associate professor at Kent State University, where he teaches literacy education courses at the graduate and undergraduate levels. A former high school English teacher, Bill has presented nationally and internationally, with over 40 articles and book chapters to his credit; his profiles of pioneering teachers comprised his book *New Literacies in Action* (2005). In November 2007, Bill began a three-year term as director of the Commission on Media for the National Council of Teachers of English. Bill continues to work in video and film and has earned a regional Emmy nomination for Outstanding Music Composition. He blogs at www.williamkist.com and can be followed on Twitter at http://twitter.com/williamkist.

To all the teachers profiled in this book
And
To Stephanie (who forms, with me, my favorite social network),
I dedicate this book.

1

The Writing Is on the Screen

Social Networking Is Here to Stay

Picture intermission at a Broadway show. The curtain has just come down after a rousing end-of-Act-One number. The lights are coming up. Suddenly, almost in unison, many people in the audience reach in their pockets or purses and flip open cell phones. Immediately, there is the sound in the air of various versions of the burning questions that seem to be on everyone's mind: "Where are you?" or "What are you doing?"

Picture afterschool at an elementary school somewhere in the Midwest. The kids are racing for their book bags and coats. As they make their way out of the building, a metamorphosis occurs as they whip out cell phones, Blackberries, iPods, and even laptops. The kids are getting back in touch with the world after hours of forced disconnect.

Picture a woman giving birth. She is in the last stages of labor and surrounded by medical staff and a loving husband who winces at her occasional cries. Periodically, between contractions, she reaches for her cell phone and posts a message to Twitter, providing her followers an account of the debut of her new son.

Variations of these pictures are taking place throughout the world at an astounding pace. One could make the argument that never before have we been more connected. The Internet has always been interactive in nature, but this latest iteration of the Internet (known as "Web 2.0") has featured an intensified level of what has come to be called "social networking." This kind of community building across interest groups, demographics, and nationalities has transformed the way we connect with strangers, loved ones, friends, colleagues, and even ourselves.

But has it transformed the way we "do" school? Attempting to answer this question is the goal of this book. How are teachers and students incorporating these new literacies that add an intensified level of social networking into their classrooms? What happens when our classrooms become as big as the world?

Terminology and Trends

What exactly do I mean by "new literacies" and "social networking"? Ah, there is the rub. We have multiple terms for these multiple literacies, and while everyone seems to know what we're talking about, no one seems to be able to agree upon what to call it. Whatever we call these new ways of communicating (new literacies, multiliteracies, ICT, media literacy, digital literacies, or multimodalities, to name a few terms being used currently), it's clear that we are experiencing a vast transformation of the way we "read" and "write," and a broadening of the way we conceptualize "literacy." As Gunther Kress (2003) has described, we are going from a page-based society to a screen-based society—a great deal of the reading and writing we do today is on a computer screen, and the texts we are accessing there include not only print communication but also elements of graphic design, video, sound, visual art, and even advertising (thus making them "multimodal"). For purposes of clarity in this book, the terms "new literacies" and "new media" will be used interchangeably to suggest not only the multimodality of today's communication forms but also the interactivity that is embedded in them—these are essentially screen-based literacies.

social networking

When I use the term *social networking* in this book, I will intend it to mean the kind of communication that takes place online using some kind of platform (Web site) such as Facebook, Twitter, or Ning in which people can place messages and connect with others who are on the Web site. These platforms usually require each participant to publish a "profile" that usually includes a picture of the participant as well as any personal details the participant wants to share, thus forming an online identity that can be wholly created by the participant. The "networking" part of social networking comes from the fact that these platforms usually involve some kind of grouping or categorization system so that we all become participants in a kind of "Kevin Bacon Game," connecting to many various "friends" and "followers" in different ways and forming networks that range in size and scope from the very small and personal to the vast, international, and professional.

These new media often allow for a great deal of interactivity (social networking); for instance, readers are able to shape a text as it is collaboratively written (even as they are simultaneously instant messaging 10 of their friends and commenting on Twitter or Facebook as to how things are going). According to the Pew Internet and American Life Project (2008), 62% of Americans are

> part of a wireless, mobile population that participates in digital activities away from home or work. Teens are creating and sharing material on the Internet in greater numbers, with 28% of online teens maintaining their own blogs. . . . Virtually, all American teens play computer, console, or cell phone games and . . . the gaming experience is rich and varied, with a significant amount of social interaction and potential for civic engagement. (Pew Internet and American Life Project, 2008)

People are tethering themselves to each other, crisscrossing the Web as they Twitter everything from the mundane to the sublime.

Twitter

Twitter is an online social network that asks participants to update their "followers" as to what they are doing in fewer than 140 characters. Some "twits" choose to "tweet" many times a day to hundreds, sometimes thousands, of followers.

SELECTED TWITTER QUOTES, 2008

- I can feel my pulse through my eye.
- What a disappointing poptart.
- I love the smell of pineapple juice.
- Just finished mowing my lawn . . . half the clippings seem to have made it into my shoes or gotten in my nose.
- Debating whether i should go to the pool today or relax in air conditioning . . . what do you think?
- 2 days till i leave for africa; 1000 things to do; new school head etc. all want mtings; am hit with worst gastro illness in memory! blah
- Tearing myself away from the computer for a bit to eat a late dinner and change out of work clothes.
- Trying to decide whether to go grocery shopping or bowling or both.
- So now that I'm using it, let me be the 400th to confirm that yes, Google apps run very fast in Chrome.
- Okay, I need to calm down. I've only been using this thing for like 20 minutes, but I'm ready to scream I like it so much.
- Baby is head down! Starting to induce.

Many of us are familiar with MySpace and Facebook—popular social networking platforms on which people post their pictures and connect with friends as well as strangers. But it also seems that most major Web sites today have some kind of sharing function, whether it's "Listmania" on Amazon, in which people make lists of book titles for different categories, or forums for discussion on YouTube, Blockbuster, Ustream, and the Internet Movie Database; on the latter, you can find discussions on everything from whether a certain actor is going bald to whether the ending of a certain film makes sense. All these spaces allow for some community to form, even if for only a few seconds. One could make the argument that today's kids are more connected to other people on a second-by-second basis than they have been at any other time in our history. These ties that bind are getting broader and more far-reaching.

The kids are definitely not alone. But we want to know whom they're not alone with—it's fine to be connected as long as they're not connecting to people who mean them harm. This fear factor may be a major reason why the social networking aspects of Web 2.0 haven't infiltrated their way into today's classroom and why they remain mainly afterschool activities (except in some of the classrooms in this book). The children are increasingly leaving our watchful care without even leaving home. They are "meeting" and talking with people whom they will probably never meet face-to-face. This is a frightening idea to educators and many adults.

The Myth of a "Safe" Adolescence

Ironically, the attempt to achieve a protected childhood is a relatively recent development. It wasn't too long ago that children took an active part in the adult world from a very young age. Before the onset of the construct of "adolescence," even into the late 1800s, "the young were often left to fend for themselves. There was very little schooling, endemic child labor, and puberty marked the moment when the fight for survival began in earnest" (Savage, 2007, p. 10). Children were put to work early not only in so-called legitimate work as factory work and agriculture but also in more questionable lines of work such as show business and even criminal pursuits such as theft and prostitution (Lahr, 1969/2000; Mintz, 2004).

The very first Puritan settlers of North America in the 1600s felt that childhood was at best a time to prepare children for death by making sure they had salvation; "children were adults in training who needed to be prepared for salvation and inducted into the world of work as early as possible" (Mintz, 2004, p. 10). Children were even shown corpses and executions so that they would have a heightened sensitivity to the reality of their own mortality; the Puritan childhood was so brutal that some children who were abducted by Native Americans preferred to stay with their captors once they were rescued (Mintz, 2004).

In the late 1800s, the writer and photographer Jacob Riis and other writers began to document the difficult lives that so many children lived; before long, there came an attempt to standardize what the typical adolescence should look like—this new "intermediate state that as yet had no name" (Savage, 2007, p. 13). The trend became one of an idealized, sanitary childhood, one in which even play was moderated, and children had to be protected from having bad lunchroom manners and driving too fast on prom night (Smith, 1999). Those in non-Western societies continued to see children as competent at a much earlier age than did those in Western societies, allowing play to proceed without formal supervision. For example, children in Western societies were increasingly subjected to a more structured, scripted childhood and adolescence (Chudacoff, 2007). Currently, it is common to hear reports of "helicopter parents," who talk with their children on the phone several times a day, hovering over their daily lives well into early adulthood. We have had several instances recently, at the university where I teach, of parents showing up for advising appointments with their children who are now graduate students!

To borrow a media phrase from the 1960s, "We've come a long way, baby!" since the 1800s. Or have we really? We may have an assumption that childhood is safer now than in those prescript days, but of course, that assumes everyone is following the script. Fast-forward to the beginning of the 21st century, and we see statistics that make it a stretch to believe that childhood is much more of a protected space for kids than it was "back in the day." According to *American's Children in Brief* (ChildStats.gov, 2008), "in 2006, 17% of all children ages 0–17 lived in poverty," and the poverty rate was higher for nonwhite children, with 33% of black children and 27% of Hispanic children living in poverty. Only 68% of children lived with two parents in 2006, down from 77% in 1980. While 88% of adults, age 18–24, had achieved a high school diploma in 2006, 26% of 12th graders described themselves as "heavy drinkers," 22% of 12th graders reported illicit drug use in the last 30 days, and almost half of students in Grades 9–12 responded that they were no longer virgins (ChildStats.gov., 2008). We may have abolished child labor, but it's not clear that our children are any better protected or any safer now than they were a century ago.

The Script at School

Whether or not there has ever truly been a scripted, "safe" childhood outside of school, there can be no doubt that since the publication of 1983's *A Nation at Risk*, there has been an increasing climate of scripted, standardized curricula and assessments inside of school, with few of these models including room for new literacies activities that fully use the potential of Web 2.0. Many districts have instituted "curriculum maps" that include fairly specific directions regarding what material is to be "covered" and at what point during the year, and while it's been demonstrated that many U.S. state standards documents include mention of new media (Kubey & Baker, 1999), many teachers still claim they don't "have room" in their daily classroom practices to explore this mandate.

Often, it is the new teachers who get caught in the squeeze between their knowledge of new media practices outside of school and the realities of rules that have been set up in school. A former student who is now a first-year teacher, Cassie Neumann, describes how wired her students are outside of school:

> As soon as 2:15 hits, they're all out and walking down the halls texting or making calls. Just today, I told a kid to put away his cell phone because I thought he was texting, but he showed me that he was actually accessing the Internet from his phone—he was on task! The rule at our school is no cell phones, no iPods, so I had him put it away, but I personally think we (a general educational "we" not meaning my district specifically) should work towards ways to integrate this technology into our classroom. I think we definitely need rules for this technology and how it is to be used in a school setting, but I think that by ignoring and banning new tech products, we are sending the wrong message.

In some cases, a disinclination to use new media in the classroom may simply stem from uncertainty and limited familiarity with the possibilities. Even the newest teachers who are supposedly "digital natives" (Prensky, 2005) may feel baffled about the plethora of new communication tools that are available and how to make best use of them in the classroom. Recently, a teacher who appeared to be in her late twenties approached me after a presentation I gave and said, "I'm embarrassed to ask, but you referred to a 'wiki' in your presentation, and I don't know what a 'wiki' is." Just because teachers and their students are relatively young (born after 1985, let's say), that is no guarantee that they are able to communicate effectively using new media. So, whether due to scripted curricula that leave no room for new media or whether due to schools' fears of new media or educators' lack of knowledge, many students are left to do their networking after school, often without adult supervision.

The Structure of This Book

This book takes the stand that the writing is on the wall or rather on the screen: Schools are going to have to move past whatever barriers exist and closer to the literacy practices increasingly used in the "outside world." No matter where you may be on the continuum of believing in or disbelieving the construct of "childhood," there can be no doubt that communicating in this new century is going to be different than communicating in the old century—not necessarily better or worse but different—and that it is going to involve some form of social networking on screen with strangers as well as friends and colleagues. Many of the teachers portrayed in this book are of the opinion that we need to give kids practice using these new media in school, where there can be a dialogue about all the issues that come up when communicating in these new ways.

But this is not a cheerleading book in which glowing portraits are provided of the transformative power of Web 2.0. This book, rather, aims to chronicle the sometimes messy first steps of educators who are attempting to include social networking inside real schools and who are grappling with all the challenges that come along with this new kind of teaching. These pioneering teachers, whom I have found through my own online social network, are attempting to figure out ways to keep their students safe while at the same time provide them with the experiences they will need to become fully functional literate citizens in this century.

The chapters are organized to parallel the various technology levels of the school environments within which the teachers I've interviewed are working and are titled in honor of the wired Starbucks terms for their different serving sizes. Thus, I begin with the most basic nonwired situation—"Short" (Chapter 2)—and lead up to those truly visionary classrooms—"Venti" (Chapter 5)—that may not look anything like the traditional chalkboard classrooms of our collective past. In between are "Tall" (Chapter 3), or a moderately limited environment, and "Grande" (Chapter 4), or a high-tech environment. It's worth noting that the size of the container, however, doesn't influence the taste of the coffee—it's all good. It is my hope that this structure—starting with examples of social networking in a low-tech environment (including my own classroom) and proceeding gradually to the most advanced levels of classroom capacity and administrative tolerance for technological innovation—will enable you to easily locate your district on this continuum and readily identify those activities that are most appropriate to try in your own school or classroom.

To provide an additional cup of reality, all of the teachers profiled in this book are teaching new media lessons within the context of standardized curricula and assessments. The constant tension between going where the kids need to go and the need to stay within a proscribed curriculum is a real-world constraint that will be discussed throughout the book. These teachers' own words provide a running commentary throughout and, mimicking blog entries, will appear in boxes at various locations in the chapters.

And I'm including my own journey toward attempting Web 2.0 projects in my own classroom of preservice teachers. Most of the work from my classroom is featured in Chapter 2 in which I provide activities that get at questions about new literacies but that use very little technology in the process. My students' comments as they come to terms with how to incorporate on-screen literacies within their own teaching will also be featured in sidebars to the text.

New Literacies: Essential Questions

Within each chapter—and indeed, providing the subtitles that chart the content—are essential questions that are worth exploring in any classroom with or without technology. This follows the lead of many of the teachers in this book who believe it is the questions that are important rather than the tools we use to explore these questions. The questions actually were developed from my own pedagogical experiments as I tried to implement what I had studied in my own classroom. Such questions include, "How do new forms transform writing?" "Who is the audience for our writing in a new media age?" and "How do we form communities?"

When I began this line of inquiry in 1997, I had to come up with some way of describing what I wanted to look at. If I were truly going to find new literacies classrooms, I was going to need to have some descriptors of what a "new literacies classroom" would look like. Based on a review of the literature available at that time, I came up with five characteristics that I felt were essential to be present for me to label a classroom as a new literacies classroom (Kist, 2000):

- New literacies classrooms feature daily work in multiple forms of representation.
- In such classrooms, there are explicit discussions of the merits of using certain symbol systems in certain situations (such as when conveying a concept, advertising a product, or expressing an emotion), and the students are given many choices about the kinds of texts they read and write.
- There are think-alouds by the teacher who models working through problems using certain symbol systems such as video production, Web site design, and print writing.
- Students take part in a mix of individual and collaborative activities.
- New literacies classrooms are places of student engagement in which students report achieving a "flow" state.

I used these characteristics again as I searched for classrooms to profile for this book and then to structure the inquiry paths my own students and I would follow (as I describe in Chapter 2). The activities that I have collected over the years support inquiry questions that can each be categorized under one or more of the original five new literacies characteristics. Each chapter includes a number of these questions and supporting activities that I have adapted or that I have collected from teachers across the world. These activities are followed by some possible questions to consider with students and some brief comments about the experiences coming out of the activities from students and teachers who have used them.

I believe this book can serve a real need for educators of all grade levels (but mainly Grades 5–adult) and all subject areas and who place themselves at any point along the continuum—from those on one end who feel increasingly left out (sometimes against their will) of new media trends and those on the other who might be considered "first adopters" and embrace whatever the latest technology is in its very newest form. In summation, this book seeks to add to the emerging literature on what a truly "socially networked" classroom could look like on a daily basis. We have very little description that deals in a systematic way with how this kind of teaching can be implemented or what some of the outcomes may be. The goal of the research that has informed this book is to identify and document the processes of teaching and learning in these pioneering new media classrooms with a special focus on projects that involve some social networking. The assignments and assessments that have been collected from across the world are documented not so much via screen shots and step-by-step instructions but rather in support of essential questions that teachers and students have always been asking, even back in the "stone-age" pre-Internet eras.

Although the questions are perennial, this book serves as a snapshot in time of the current state of classroom teachers' use of screen-based literacies, through its inclusion of many real-world examples—assignment sheets, assessments, and rubrics that I have collected through online and phone interviews with teachers across the world in 2007 and 2008. These examples of real work are set in a context of the rapidly evolving world of literacy instruction. As in my earlier book (Kist, 2005), I see myself as a qualitative researcher, a reporter, and a participant, taking down oral histories at the beginning of this revolution in teaching, attempting to show how this looks now in the "real world" of K–12 classrooms. The backdrop for this study is a field that is trapped between these new developments in media and the countervailing emphasis on the standardizing and even franchising of teaching and learning. My own classroom will be included in this story, partly due to the fact that I am working with preservice teachers whom I continue to follow into the early years of their careers and who tell me that for a variety of reasons, they just aren't able to try "cutting-edge" assignments during student teaching or the first years of their fledgling careers. So, we begin at the very beginning.

2

"Short"

Social Networking in a Low-Tech Environment

Some teachers work in schools with very little technology. And some teachers work in schools that have lots of technology but choose not to use that technology, whether because they are too busy to learn something new or are just fearful. This chapter describes some activities that I adapted that can be done in a very "low-tech" environment. These activities help students explore some foundational questions that are timely for any classroom but have particular relevance to the social networking skills of our students, whether on- or off-screen.

I have a confession to make. As I was writing my first book, which was a profile of new literacies teachers, I realized I was not "walking the walk." In my scholarly life, I was attempting to be a proponent of multiliteracy reading and writing (Kist, 2000, 2003, 2005). But when it came time for me to teach actual students myself after years of being in an administrative position, now that I was teaching again at the college level, I was far from being a new literacies teacher.

What's more, I was now teaching future teachers—people who will be teaching for many years into the 21st century. I was potentially influencing pedagogical practices that would impact thousands of children as my

---

Portions of this chapter originally appeared in Kist, W. (2005). Walking the walk: New literacies in my own classroom. *Ohio Journal of English Language Arts, 46*(1), 49–57.

students graduated and taught hundreds of young people over the courses of their careers. Not only did I need to "walk the walk," I needed to pick up the pace.

Beginning in late 2002 and throughout 2003, I visited classrooms throughout the United States and Canada—from Los Angeles to Snow Lake, from Chicago to Montreal and beyond—watching some of the most visionary teachers who were immersed not only in the technology but also in the implications of using these new media in their classrooms. During my travels, I began to be quite conscious of my own less-than-current uses of technology and new educational practices; I was embarrassed that I didn't even have my own Web page. When people asked me for the URL for my Web page, I tried to cover and say that it was on my department's Web site at Kent State, and that the URL was so long I couldn't remember what it was (which was actually true). I never told people that I didn't own a computer in my home until 1996 or a cell phone until 2003.

Originally, I had become interested in this line of research because of my interest in film, not because of any particular interest in computer technology. Now, however, film was rapidly becoming an "old" medium (although very much integrated into new media), and as I was spending time chronicling the practices of the pioneers of this movement just like the silent-film stars chronicled by Brownlow (1969/1976), the parade was passing me by.

Mindful of the need to teach my lessons in the context of lessons that the preservice teachers could emulate, I reviewed all the outstanding new literacies assignments I had found and then created some myself. What follows in this chapter are descriptions of some of the assignments I have used with my students at Kent State University. Over the years of using them, I have found that they group themselves according to questions that get at some characteristics of new literacies classrooms, starting with the notion that these kinds of new literacies classrooms feature daily work in multiple forms of representation, not just occasionally, and that "reading" and "writing" these new media takes some practice and reflection.

How Have We Been Shaped by Media Experiences?

For years, I had started my courses by having students complete a "Literacy Autobiography" on paper. This assignment requires students to look back over their past reading and writing. As I became immersed in new literacies myself, I decided to broaden the assignment and get students thinking about how we have all been shaped by many kinds of texts that surround us. To model the activity for these preservice teachers, I have loaded many pictures into a PowerPoint presentation that demonstrates how my own life has been shaped by such diverse texts as sitcoms—*All in the Family,* for example—and "high art" (jazz performances by Bill Evans and works of art hanging at the Cleveland Museum of Art). As the images flash by on the screen, music starts to play, and I see moments of recognition as students witness that they and I have been influenced by some common texts even across a generation.

SELECTED ITEMS IN WILLIAM KIST'S POWERPOINT MULTIGENRE AUTOBIOGRAPHY

A *Peanuts* cartoon

Picture of Woody Allen and Mariel Hemingway in *Manhattan*

Music playing: "Watermelon Man" by Herbie Hancock

Book cover: Willa Cather's *My Ántonia*

Picture of Adam West in *Batman*

Painting: *Stag at Sharkey's* (1909) by George Bellows

TV Guide cover with Jackie Gleason

Picture of Bill Evans playing the piano

Book cover: *David Copperfield* by Charles Dickens

Picture of plastic figurine of the cartoon character *Pogo*

Picture of Stan Laurel and Oliver Hardy

Picture of Cleveland Kiddie Show TV Host "Barnaby"

Picture of Derek Jacobi in *I, Claudius*

Picture of the four main characters in *Seinfeld*

After my life has finished flashing before their eyes, I ask the students to immediately jot down texts that have been influential in their own lives—pieces of music, poetry, films, and even fashion and architecture. We share these texts with each other in a kind of freewheeling brainstorm that is equal parts nostalgia and recognition of how we are all immeasurably shaped by the various forms of communication around us. Then, I send them home to create their multigenre autobiographies. These may be turned in using multiple forms—PowerPoint, for example, or MovieMaker or iMovie. The criteria for the project's success is whether the students can demonstrate a clear link between the various texts and how their lives have been influenced by those texts. The actual assignment I give them is adapted from a couple of sources and includes suggested questions they might use to spark their thinking about different kinds of texts.

MULTIGENRE LITERACY AUTOBIOGRAPHY: THE ASSIGNMENT

This assignment encourages you to think about all the various texts of your life. Your own history as a reader and writer of various texts has a significant impact on how you "read" and "write" today. Thinking about the following questions and creating a multimodal artifact should help you reflect on your own multigenre literacy of today.

Below are some prompts to help you get started writing your multigenre literacy autobiography:

1. What are your earliest recollections of reading and writing?
2. What are your earliest recollections of watching television?
3. What are your earliest recollections of going to see a film?
4. What are your earliest recollections of music?
5. What are your earliest recollections of using a computer?
6. Were you read to as a child?
7. Before you were able to read, did you pretend to read books? Can you remember the first time you read a book?
8. What pleasures or problems do you associate with early memories of reading and writing?
9. What kinds of texts have you preferred over your life?
10. Was a newspaper delivered to your home? Do you recall seeing others read the newspaper? Did you read the newspaper?
11. How did pop culture (movies, TV, music, Internet) impact your literacy and vice versa?
12. How did your gender, race, social class, and/or ethnicity impact your reading ability, what you read, and/or your attitude toward reading?
13. Did you subscribe to children's magazines? Did your parents or siblings have magazine subscriptions?
14. Did your parents belong to a book club? Did they maintain a personal library? Did they read for pleasure?
15. Can you recall seeing family members making lists and receiving and sending mail?

16. Did you receive and send mail (such as birthday cards, thank-you notes, letters) when you were a child?
17. Can you remember any other indications that reading and writing were valued in the environment in which you grew up?
18. Can you detail your first memories of reading and writing instruction? Materials used? Methods of teaching? Content?
19. Can you remember how alternative (nonprint) texts were used at school, if at all?
20. How were computers used (or not used) during your educational journey?
21. Can you recall reading for pleasure in elementary school?
22. Can you remember writing for pleasure in elementary school?
23. Can you recall the first book you chose to read in elementary school?
24. Can you recall your first writing assignment in elementary school?
25. Did you have a library card when you were in elementary school? Did you use it then? What predominantly did you check out from the library? In later school years?
26. Can you recall the first book you loved (couldn't put down)?
27. Can you recall the first film or television show you loved and watched over and over again?
28. Do you feel that you've ever read a book that has made a difference in your life?
29. Has a nonprint text made a difference in your life?
30. Have you ever read a book that you knew had been challenged or censored? How did you feel about reading it?
31. Have you ever encountered a text online that you thought adults would be upset to know that you encountered? How did you feel about encountering that text?
32. Were you a reader in your intermediate and/or junior high or middle school years?
33. How did your reading and writing habits change when you went to school and over the years?

(Continued)

(Continued)

34. Are there any social, cultural, and/or religious organizations associated with writing or reading that you recall?
35. Can you pleasurably recall sharing books with friends?
36. Can you pleasurably recall talking about nonprint texts with friends?
37. Did you read a certain type of book (such as mysteries or biographies) at a particular age? Why do you think you made such choices?
38. Were you required to read certain novels in middle school or high school? How did you feel about that?
39. What is your all-time favorite children's book? What is your favorite book that you've read as an adult?
40. Have you ever seen a book you've read turned into a film?
41. Have there been times in your life when you have viewed reading as a pleasurable activity?
42. Have there been times in your life when you have viewed writing as a pleasurable activity?
43. Is there a specific teacher (or several) who stands out in your memory as someone who had an impact on your reading and/or writing?
44. What contributions have your reading and writing abilities made to your life?
45. Are you a reader now?
46. Are you a writer now?
47. What alternative media do you peruse most often now?
48. Do you feel comfortable modeling reading and writing for your students?
49. What are you currently reading? Writing?

Source: Adapted by William Kist from McLaughlin & Vogt (1996) and Brown (1999).

Because this assignment is given very early in the course, I don't suggest much of a structure or even medium for turning in their literacy autobiographies. I tell them they can turn in the assignment in whichever medium they prefer—from writing an essay, to shooting a video, to doing a PowerPoint presentation. Because nervous students always want to know how they're being graded (and because they deserve to know), I do present them with a very simple list of criteria.

MULTIGENRE LITERACY AUTOBIOGRAPHY: EVALUATION CRITERIA

For this assignment, you will be evaluated on the following criteria:

- *Thoughtfulness of your response:* Does your autobiography appear to have been just thrown together at the last minute or has some real thought gone into it?
- *Thoroughness of your examination of your literacy past:* Have you used a variety of texts to represent different eras of your life?
- *Insights into the influences of your literacy history on your life:* Have you drawn conclusions as to how the various media texts have influenced your life?

You will not be evaluated on mechanics issues or technical proficiency in whatever medium you are using.

As we debrief the assignment, students enjoy the reminiscing but also begin to realize how deeply all these texts are embedded in their memories and how much the media, both print and nonprint, are tied to their life experiences. Many students talk about the first film they attended or how excited they were to check a book out of the library for the first time or how excited they were to meet Bert and Ernie in person when they were taken to see *Sesame Street: Live!*

As we talk about these important texts in our lives, both print and nonprint, we start writing recurring themes on the board—themes of establishing identity; the power of autobiography; how certain texts, such as books, seem privileged; and the evident increasing influence of a screen-based literacy (Kress, 2003; Schofield & Rogers, 2004). We talk about the broad spectrum of literary practices—everything from getting a library card to creating a password—that make up our literacy lives (Barton & Hamilton, 1998).

Beyond the issues revolving around new literacies that this activity brings out, there are also qualities of the assignment itself that students begin to notice. This early in the course, students already are talking about how addicting these kinds of assignments are. Many students admit to sitting at their computers working for hours assembling their multigenre autobiographies. After we exhibit them, many students go back to add more content to their own autobiographies because their memories have been stimulated by what their peers have done.

How Do New Forms Shape Reading and Writing?

For many years, I did the first of the next activities as a fun way of helping kids to sequence—put the events of a story in order. The

Garmston and Wellman (1992) activity is a silent game in which students attempt to line up in order of their birthdays, finding their correct places in line without talking, communicating only in sign language. Once this task has been accomplished, it can be used to teach sequencing by having students put the events of a story on note cards or sticky notes that they affix to their shirts and then place themselves in the order that the events follow in the story. At the end of the activity, the class has formed itself in a straight line that traces the events of the story.

ACTIVITY ONE: HOW DO WE READ IN A "NONLINEAR" WAY?

Ask students to line up in a straight line facing the teacher.

1. At the signal, students are to reassemble in the order of their birthdays, starting with January birthdays all the way to the December birthdays at the end of the line. Students aren't to give their years of birth—this isn't an exercise in age!
2. As students are doing this, they are not to talk. They may communicate using hand signals.
3. Once students have lined up in order of their birthdays, have a discussion about what linearity means.
4. Next, place the events of a story on note cards and give one to each student. The students must arrange themselves in order of the events, again without talking.
5. Walk down the line from left to right and demonstrate how we usually read a book from beginning to end.
6. Go back to the beginning of the line and demonstrate how we read in a nonlinear fashion. Walk down the line until you get to the fourth or fifth person, then jump to the 10th person and walk down the line for a little while until you get to the 16th person, then jump back to the first person, then back to person the 20th, and so on. Explain to the students that this is the way people read in a nonlinear fashion.

Source: Adapted from Garmston & Wellman, 1992.

After the activity, I walk down the line from left to right, demonstrating how we traditionally read a book from beginning to end. Then, I go back to the beginning of the line and start bopping around in random fashion, walking down the line for a while, then jumping to the end, then back to the beginning, then to the middle, thus signifying nonlinear reading. We then brainstorm about how nonlinear reading is different than linear reading. What does it mean to the author of a screen-based (Web-based) text when there is no ability to predict how the reader will read that text?

Of course, it could be argued that we have always had the ability to read texts in a nonlinear fashion by reading the last page first, for example. Many students mention how they read the final chapter of the final Harry Potter book first because they wanted to find out if he lived. Or the plot of a book may also be organized in a nonlinear way, with flashbacks and flash-forwards. Sometimes when students are still lined up, I demonstrate how some works deliberately place the last chronological event first in the story, such as *Citizen Kane* with the opening scene of the protagonist on his deathbed. This opens up a discussion of flashbacks, made so popular now by the television series *Lost* and *Heroes*. So it has probably always been appropriate to talk about the nonlinearity of "reading" texts, but with more texts now being screen-based and embedded with hyperlinks, this distinction between nonlinear and linear reading is more appropriate for discussion than ever.

QUESTIONS TO CONSIDER

1. Think about how you normally read a book. Do you normally read it from beginning to end, or do you sometimes skip to the end?
2. How do you think it changes the writer's task when the text being written will be read in random order—for example, a Web site?
3. How is reading on the Web different than reading a book?
4. Do you prefer one style of reading?
5. Does it confuse you or entertain you to read a text that seems to proceed in random order? What might the author's purpose be for writing something in a nonlinear fashion (such as in films such as *Citizen Kane* and *Crash*)?

I have used the next assignment to get students to think about how to create hybrid texts. Since so many new media texts contain elements of different forms of representation, it is worth exploring with students how hybrid texts become more than the sum of their parts. This simple assignment can be adapted to many different texts—it obviously isn't confined to *Julius Caesar*!

ACTIVITY TWO: JULIUS CAESAR, THE MUSICAL

The objective of this assignment is to provide the students with a reason to go back and look over the play *Julius Caesar* by William Shakespeare, which they have just finished reading. This helps them see it as a unified entity, as a theatrical work that Shakespeare wrote with playgoers in mind, as a story that progresses from ideas to action to results, as a literary work that explores both internal and external conflict. Students must select five musical works, one for each act of the play. Each musical selection should reflect an event, incident, character, or mood in that particular act. Musical selections must be school appropriate, but they may represent any musical genre. For example, "The King's March" by Jeremiah Clarke could be used for Caesar's triumphal march into Rome in Act I, Buddy Miller's "Worry Too Much" could convey Brutus's internal conflict at the beginning of Act II, and "Belle Watling" from the *Gone With the Wind* soundtrack could represent the sadness of Portia's death as Brutus reveals it as the source of his emotional outburst in Act IV. Students should be prepared to share their selections with the class.

Source: From Karen Barta, Black River High School.

"It allowed me to take a risk. I am not usually an artistic person." —Diane

Tom Romano's multigenre paper project is another similar way of getting kids to think across genres as they are writing on a defined topic (Romano, 1995, 2000). In a multigenre paper, students must write in several different genres—such as an obituary, a journal entry, a painting, a song—as they explore a certain topic, such as "Injustice in the American West" or "Growing Up in China." Having students create a hybrid text, such as "Julius Caesar, the Musical," or a multigenre paper gets them thinking about how works of art in different media still get at some of the same themes and that, in a new media age, many texts we encounter contain multiple forms of representation (music, print, image) within the same text. Sometimes, after students are given the freedom to create these kinds of hybrid texts, they continue to ask if they can add music that they themselves create or some visual art they have made in reaction to a page-based text. Other students report being challenged by the experience of working in hybrid forms.

"I got the opportunity to play with art, which is something I don't usually do." —Ariel

QUESTIONS TO CONSIDER

1. How did it change your opinion of *Julius Caesar* (or whatever text you used) when you added music to it?
2. What can "hybrid" texts get across that a text written in a single genre cannot? What can single-genre texts do that hybrid texts cannot?

3. Would you prefer to create a hybrid text rather than a single-genre piece? If so, why?
4. What are some examples of texts that could be considered hybrid?

When we talk about "hybrid texts," that often leads to pulling the components of that hybrid apart and focusing on the different forms of representation that make up the whole. This can lead to a discussion of the affordances with each medium. I often start this discussion with the form that brought me into the new literacies research in the first place: film, an inherently hybrid text that includes speech, music, and images.

How Do We Respond to Film Texts?

Helping kids learn to respond to texts is probably one of the most crucial tasks we need to accomplish with them. With print texts, many students, sadly, are stuck at the decoding stage, just struggling to make sense of whatever text they are reading. But for those students who get past the decoding stage, there is the question, "Now what?" This response process gets more complicated when we are now responding to both page-based and screen-based texts and when our response itself can be formed using both page-based and screen-based texts.

My interest in new literacies really was generated when I started showing short silent films to my high school English students. As a new teacher, I struggled with how to make the literary canon that I was expected to teach relatable to the urban teenagers I was working with. Because of my own love of film, I stumbled upon using silent films in my language arts classroom. One of the most memorable moments I had as a teacher was showing my students Charlie Chaplin's *The Kid*, a silent film that was made in 1921. This silent film traces the ups and downs of Chaplin's attempts to help an orphan child of about six or seven, played by child star Jackie Coogan. I showed it to my students one day because film as a genre was tangentially mentioned in my curriculum but mainly because I loved it and wanted to show it off to an audience that had never seen a silent film. I was soon amazed to see how my students loved it too. They were transfixed by the story, especially at the part in the film when the child welfare authorities come to take the child away from Chaplin. I saw my tough urban kids melt as the orphan boy is thrown in the police wagon and taken away, leaving Chaplin desolate. The kids were truly engrossed in the film. This classroom experience with a Chaplin film was one of those moments that teachers have when we know we are onto something big. That one teaching moment is one of the key events in my career that has led to the book that you are reading at this very moment.

I knew that my students were responding to this film, and I knew that they could also respond to Shakespeare and Dickens, and I knew that they could respond to Miles Davis and Jackson Pollock and all the other great artists who create texts. In my classroom, I began to break down the hierarchy of texts, so that we discussed Poe's "The Cask of Amontillado" at the same time we discussed *The Addams Family*. Before I even went to graduate school to learn what I was doing, I was creating a postmodern classroom with the result that, to this day, I run into former students who comment on how they still remember some of the things we did. I ran into one of my former students recently who wondered if I still had a copy of the video adaptation they had done—an urban street video version of "The Knight's Tale" from Chaucer's *Canterbury Tales*. Fortunately, I did still have a copy of their video, and I burned a copy for him. He and his group of friends now have careers in business and law enforcement, but he later told me they regressed to their teen years when they got together to watch their old video—work they had not seen in 10 years. I always think of this story when I hear people suggesting that the new media are "dumbing down" the curriculum—I challenge any British literature teacher to name a project that would have the students still talking about Chaucer 10 years later.

But I betray my print-centric background as an English teacher, as I talk about returning to Chaucer. A breaking down of this kind of hierarchy of symbol systems probably begins by helping kids to respond to texts, both print and nonprint—and not necessarily tied to print texts—in a thoughtful manner. To launch such a discussion, I use an activity I took from noted media educator Frank Baker of the Media Literacy Clearinghouse (http://www.frankwbaker.com/default1.htm).

ACTIVITY ONE: ANALYZING FILMS ELEMENT BY ELEMENT

Show the students the first seven minutes of Steven Spielberg's *E.T.: The Extra-Terrestrial* with no introduction. All they have to do is watch the clip. After the clip is done, break them into small groups, and give each group a "Film Analysis Card" with printed directions that ask them to watch the clip again but to concentrate on one element of the film production.

Lighting

What time of day is it?

What are the clues?

What effect does lighting have?

Use two or three adjectives to describe the lighting.

Sound Effects

Close your eyes.

You are only to listen to the scene, after which you will be asked to make a list of everything you heard and then share.

Music

Describe the music at the beginning, middle, and end of the scene.

What happens and why?

How does the music contribute to the mood or feel?

Is the music effective?

What might happen if there were no music in this scene? How would that impact your impressions?

Camera: Movement

Document when the director or cinematographer uses the following:

Pan (left or right move)

Tilt (up or down move)

A crane shot (high above)

What is the purpose of these actions?

Editing

Count the number of edits in this scene. What impact does editing have?

Camera: Lens

Document when the director or cinematographer uses the following:

Wide shot

Medium shot

Close up

Zoom in or out

Why does he or she use these shots when he or she does?

Mood

What mood does this scene put you in?

How do you feel?

Why do you feel this way?

What has the director done to push your emotional buttons? (Be specific.)

Just by asking students to concentrate on one element of a film, it opens their eyes to see how many formal elements go into the production of the film and that a film can indeed be looked at as formally as can a sonnet or a painting. Students report that it is difficult to go back to watching films casually after looking at scenes in a very focused way after doing this exercise. Sometimes students confess that they didn't realize that watching movies "counts" as participating in a serious art form. Frank reports, "It is my experience that students are most anxious to share what they now see, hear, and feel" after doing this activity. "It is empowering to hear their newly discovered understandings of what the director of the film was attempting to do."

Similarly, Heidi Whitus, communications teacher at Communications Arts High School in San Antonio, uses specific prompts to help her students think about different aspects of a film's message and appeal. She uses the following prompts to get her students thinking and writing analytically about film as a medium worthy of thoughtful response.

ACTIVITY TWO: FILM PROMPTS

- We watched several films in class in which the main characters are not exactly "good guys." Unlike George, the quintessential "good guy" in *It's a Wonderful Life*, they violate basic societal rules on a daily basis. Think of another film you have seen (*not* one we have watched in class) in which the protagonist is a bad person in the eyes of traditional society yet is still a likeable character. Describe how you felt about the character; what made that character "bad," and how did the film resolve the issue (think about what happened to the main characters in *The Public Enemy* and *Bonnie and Clyde*).
- Westerns are easily identifiable by their location: typically the American West, usually in the 19th century. However, some of the markers that identify a Western can be found in films with different settings. Describe a film you have seen that has the markers of a Western but takes place elsewhere. Explain the markers that make this film a "Western."
- Compare and contrast a remake of a horror classic with its original (e.g., *Psycho*, *The Haunting*, *The Fog*, and many more). Write 200 words in which you explain which version you thought was a more interesting and effective film. Consider such factors as the following:

  o how the film was changed to satisfy a different audience,
  o technological developments since the original, and
  o our society's evolving standards for how much gore and violence is acceptable (or required) in a horror film.

  Alternate question for those who have not seen any horror film remakes:

- We are viewing four black-and-white films in a row in class (*The Cabinet of Dr. Caligari*, *Bride of Frankenstein*, *Psycho*, and *The Haunting*). Many people say they hate black-and-white films; others love them. Describe how you feel about black-and-white films compared to color films and whether your opinion is changing as you get older. Use specific films you have seen as examples.

- *The Abominable Dr. Phibes* is considered a cult classic, a film that has a small but devoted body of fans. Describe the elements of this film that you believe make it beloved by some fans but at the same time prevent it from achieving wider popularity.
- Also, if you have any favorite "cult classic" films, talk about them here.
- *New requirement*: In addition to your initial response of *at least 150 words*, you must also *respond* to at least one of your classmates. This means that you must have at least two entries for this week.

Source: From Heidi Whitus, Communications Arts High School, San Antonio, Texas.

What Does It Mean to Represent an Idea Visually?

Once we have looked at the moving image, we begin to look at the static image. Many English teachers (and other subject matter teachers) may believe that this kind of activity is more fitting for art class. In English class, we have traditionally focused on the printed word as our communication medium. Both the reading and writing of print have been the focus of this field since it began around the beginning of the 20th century (Eagleton, 1983). Now, we face an age in which we are shifting to a screen-based society (Kress, 2003) in which much of our reading will be from a screen, and therefore, reading will not only encompass print but also images, sound, and motion as well. Visual literacy skills should be included if we truly want to prepare students for this new kind of reading. I think many teachers approach this by looking at paintings and visual art, and I have done this also. But I have also used a very old parlor game that has been suggested by Jeffrey Wilhelm (1997) to get kids visually representing what they read.

SNAPSHOT OR TABLEAUX DRAMAS

1. Form students into groups of three to five and assign each of them a scene from a book, a historical event, or a scientific process.
2. Explain that each group is going to have to visually represent this event somehow using their bodies. That is to say, they will not be permitted to draw a picture or use sign language. They must somehow reenact the event in such a way that it is somewhat recognizable.
3. Groups should be given time to "rehearse."

(Continued)

(Continued)

4. Once they are ready to perform, each group will take the stage and freeze in a tableaux representing the event they are supposed to be depicting.
5. A variation on the activity allows audience members, if they can't guess what the event being depicted is, to ask one or more of the actors "yes or no" questions about what is being represented.

Source: Adapted from Wilhelm, 1997.

One of the main reactions I get when doing this activity is from the shy students—they just feel uncomfortable standing up before the class and representing some scene with their bodies. Of course, there are many outgoing students who may even have some theatrical experience who love such an activity. So this opens up a discussion (after the students are done presenting their tableaux) about what we can do as teachers to make our classrooms places in which all students can thrive no matter what their modality of choice is for expressing themselves. What is the point of trying to represent an idea or an event visually?

QUESTIONS TO CONSIDER

1. Discuss the challenges of this activity. Are there some things that are more difficult to represent visually?
2. Why would someone decide to represent something visually?
3. Is a picture *really* worth a thousand words?
4. Think about a time in your life when you have appreciated having a picture of something more than you might have appreciated having words to describe it.
5. Think about a time in your life when you were glad to have words. What are the commonalities between the things we tend to represent verbally and the things we represent visually? What are the differences?
6. What were your feelings about getting up and presenting your tableaux in front of the class?

What Does "Genre" Mean, Particularly When We Are Working Across Texts?

Genre study has been a mainstay of the English classroom for many years. Whether creating entire courses or units around genres such as science fiction or mysteries or grouping literature circles around genres, language arts teachers often have stressed the features of various genres—both from the standpoint of the reader's needing to recognize certain conventions that are identified with certain genres and from the standpoint of the writer's need to compose within certain genre principles. Reading teachers also have focused on genre as a way of organizing and aiding the process of independent reading. Learning how to judge what a book will be about just from its cover comes back to a genre study of book covers.

But what happens to genres in a multimodal world? Are there characteristics of a genre such as horror, for example, that cut across forms of representation? Are there, on the other hand, certain elements of the horror film that don't translate to the horror novel? In a new media world, the genres and forms of communication keep multiplying so quickly that one could be discussing a new form practically every week, so perhaps it's worth having a discussion of certain elements of certain genres that seem to stand up no matter the time period and no matter the form of representation.

TEXT COMPARISONS ACROSS GENRES

1. Bring in examples of any two forms of communication—anything from a poem to an advertisement to the main page of a Web site. Try to use texts that both come from the same genre—horror, for example—but that are in different text forms (a Stephen King novel and the film *Psycho*, for example).

   1a. Expand the activity to a third form of communication and so on.

2. Brainstorm with students as to the similarities and/or differences between forms of communication: What can be done with digital communication that can't be done with print (page-based) communication? What can be done with page-based communication that can't be done with digital media?
3. Begin an ongoing list of characteristics of various genres and forms of communication.

These discussions sometimes lead to huge bulletin boards that stay up the entire semester in which students begin to list all of the texts that fit with a certain genre. Students can add to the genre lists over a period of time as they encounter new texts that fit within any of the genres. Informal discussions that compare and contrast the different texts within any genre may lead to a more formalized response or may stay at the level of conversation. An interesting next step is to talk about whether there are certain genres that have less fluid elements—elements that stay intact no matter the text.

QUESTIONS TO CONSIDER

1. What are the common elements of the horror genre or any genre, and how do they translate into the different forms of communication?
2. Are there certain genre-specific elements that don't translate well across forms—that are more form specific? If so, why?
3. Speculate as to how an artist makes a decision on which form to use to express himself or herself.

What Is the Power Behind Listing and Classifying Texts?

The pleasure that students have with the previous assignment can lead to a discussion of two key elements of new media activities: assembly and categorization. We are increasingly using new media as digital scrapbooks of our lives, whether sharing our favorite pictures on Flickr or creating a list of our favorite screwball comedies on Amazon's Listmania. Over the years, I have always set up my students with some kind of reading and writing portfolio and have generally followed the model Nancie Atwell (1998) describes. One of the first minilessons Atwell advocates teaching is her "Reading and Writing Territories" activity, in which the entire class, including the teacher, starts keeping lists of all the reading they do and all of the writing. I assign a similar activity, but I broaden it to include categories that Atwell did not, categories that take into account new media.

TEXT CATEGORIES ACTIVITY

1. Give students a list of categories, such as the following:

   Favorite Authors of Fiction

   Favorite Poets

   Favorite Authors for Adolescents

   Favorite Filmmakers

   Favorite Musicians

   Favorite Visual Artists

   Favorite Dancers

   Favorite Web Sites

   Favorite Video Game

Favorite Blog

Favorite Graphic Novel

2. Model how you would respond to some of the categories above.
3. Ask students to create a document that has these categories (and any others they want to add) and then keep the document open and add to it throughout the year.
4. Give students another list of categories, this time related to writing:

   Topics

   Genres

   Audiences

5. Model how you would respond to some of the categories above, making sure to emphasize under "Genres" that all writing "counts," such as texting, IMing, and even writing sticky notes.
6. Ask students to create a document that has these categories (and any others they want to add) and then keep the document open and add to it throughout the year.

Source: Adapted from Atwell, 1998.

QUESTIONS TO CONSIDER

1. What is your reaction after having seen a list of your reading territories?
2. What is your reaction after having seen a list of your writing territories?
3. Do you see any trends in your reading? What types of books do you prefer? What kinds of texts to you prefer?
4. Do you see any trends in your writing? What kinds of things do you tend to like to write about? How does the genre impact your writing?
5. What is the point of this kind of listing? Is it a waste of time?

One interesting outcome came about as a result of doing this activity. Several students wondered if they could put their lists and then their entire reading and writing portfolios online. One day, I had finished with the Listmania activity described above, and one of my students asked, "Why don't we put our reading portfolios online?" I hesitated for a moment. Why did I hesitate? I suppose the first thing that popped into my head was the security issue—would students' work be safe? I knew that over the years many of the students had written very personal things that they included in their writing portfolios. Would they still continue to write in an unguarded manner if they knew their work was going to be online somewhere? I knew also that some students occasionally read books that contained offensive words even in the titles. Since they are adults in college, this hasn't been a problem, but would it be a problem when their reading logs were online for everyone to see? Or would everyone have to see them? Could I set them up as password protected, and if so, who would get the password?

In short, in about 30 seconds many negative thoughts went through my head. I was stumped, and my student sat before me looking at me with an expression on her face that implied she was thinking, *So what's the big deal?* But of course, I punted and made the "teacherish" comment, "Let me think about it."

Fortunately, as I began to think about the implications of her request, I began to see some positive reasons for keeping the reading and writing portfolios online, especially in this more socially connected Web 2.0 world. These portfolios would be more public than they ever had been. I thought of the benefits to the students' reading and writing that could accrue if these documents were opened up to a wider audience—and not a passive audience but one that could potentially interact with the texts and even shape them. This publication of what had previously been private documents, only for the eyes of the teacher, would now be opened up potentially to the entire world. Perhaps students in other classes, in other schools, all over the globe could comment on both writing pieces and on books listed in the reading logs. Perhaps this would impact the writing severely, making students censor themselves before writing. But perhaps also this is good practice for them in making public some (or all) aspects of their personal lives.

What does "literacy" mean when it is increasingly public and collaborative?

This next group of activities supports questions that center around just that mix of individual and collaborative activities that comprise one characteristic of new literacies classrooms.

How Do We Form Communities?

After talking about our own individual identities and how they are shaped by the texts around us, we then start talking about building community with others and how these communities shape and mediate us whether we are participating in them face-to-face or virtually. I start by using two older activities that were originally designed to promote cooperative learning but can be expanded to point out elements of social networking in a Web 2.0 world. First, we do the activity called "Finding Famous Fictional Friends and Families."

COMMUNITY BUILDING

Activity One: Finding Famous Fictional Friends and Families

1. Put students in groups of three to four.
2. Give each person a 3x5 index card.
3. Ask each group to come up with three or four names that go together. The names don't have to be fictional if you don't want them to be.

   Examples: John, Paul, George, and Ringo

   Harry, Hermione, and Ron

   Barack, George, and Bill

   Marcia, Greg, Jan, and Bobby
4. Once each group has decided on a group of names, direct each person to write one of the fictional names on his or her card. For instance, in the Beatles group above, one person would write "John" on his or her card; one person would write "Paul"; one person would write "George"; and one person would write "Ringo."
5. Collect everyone's card.
6. Check to make sure you don't have two "Beatles" groups, for example, or two Harry Potter groups. For this activity to work, each group has to be a unique combination.
7. Redistribute the cards randomly.
8. Direct each student to get out of his or her seat and stand with the people whose cards "fit" with the one in his or her possession.

Adapted from Silberman, 1996.

Activity Two: Four Corners

1. Come up with 5 to 10 opinion statements.
2. Write the following code on the board:

   1 = Strongly Agree

   2 = Agree

   3 = Disagree

   4 = Strongly Disagree

   0 = Neutral

(Continued)

(Continued)

3. Direct students to number a piece of paper from one to however many statements you have.
4. Read aloud the statements and have students write the number that corresponds with how they feel.

   Example: One of the opinion statements could be, "McDonald's is a better restaurant than Burger King." If you agree with that statement, you should mark 2.
5. Once you get through reading all the statements, go around the room and mark the four corners of the room with the following labels: Strongly Agree, Agree, Disagree, and Strongly Disagree.
6. Direct students to stand up.
7. Read aloud the opinion statements again and direct students to stand in the corner that corresponds with their opinions. The students will thus group and regroup multiple times, forming different combinations with each statement read aloud.

Source: Adapted from Garmston, R. J., & Wellman, B. M. (1999). *The adaptive school: A sourcebook for developing collaborative groups.* Norwood, MA: Christopher-Gordon Publishers.

I usually start by asking students to brainstorm about what was different about the two activities, mainly focusing on how it was to form groups in these two different ways. In Activity One, students found themselves standing in a group that was completely randomly formed (based on whatever name happened to be on the card). In Activity Two, students found themselves in groups that ebbed and flowed based on the opinion statement under consideration. Students like the first activity in that it provides a purely random way of forming groups (something that may be useful to them in their future classes). But most of the conversation tends to be about the second activity as students are amazed at the commonalities and differences between the groups that form and dissipate throughout the activity. "I didn't know you like McDonald's better than Burger King," or "I didn't know you believe in capital punishment." Students like the fact that they must declare their preferences by themselves first so they are not swayed by peer pressure in any way. We explore how affinity groups form online based around common interests and how the people you meet in these groups may surprise you. This leads to a discussion of identity formation. What does it mean when you can declare your likes and dislikes in a relatively anonymous space? Does it lead to more individualism or less? Do we tend to shape our identities purposefully online in a different way than we do when communicating in person?

QUESTIONS TO CONSIDER

1. Which activity was more satisfying?
2. Which activity simulates social networking on the Internet more accurately?
3. Which activity simulates face-to-face social networking more accurately?
4. What patterns do we tend to follow when we socialize with people whether it is online or face-to-face?
5. What patterns break down when groups form truly based on common likes or dislikes, not based on demographic closeness?
6. Is there more or less freedom to be oneself online?

How Can We Work Together?

The ability to collaborate seems to be generally acknowledged as an essential in a new media environment. To approximate the collaborative spirit that needs to be present in order to be an effective communicator in these digital times, I have relied upon some old theater games that are usually played to help actors become better at improvising and coping with whatever may happen on the stage before a live audience. The actors in a play must work together as an ensemble, or the piece breaks down. The "Count to Ten" activity is one that forces a group of people to listen to each other and collaborate toward a goal.

COUNT TO TEN!

1. Direct students to form a circle. The teacher should stand outside the circle.
2. The group is directed to attempt to count to 10 (or whatever number) with members of the group randomly shouting out one number at a time.
3. Any time two members of the group shout out a number at the same time, the group must start over.
4. Group members can't use any signals or patterns to indicate when a number is going to be shouted out.
5. The group wins when they successfully count to whatever number is desired.

Source: Adapted from Loomans & Kolberg, 1993.

The most noticeable classroom element with the Count to Ten activity is the almost instant concentration it engenders in the class. Students really want to accomplish this task. There is noticeable amusement, but also frustration, when they almost get to 10 only to have to start over again when two people say the number "9," for example, simultaneously. When the group reaches its goal, there is a huge, spontaneous, loud cheer. They are truly happy to have reached the goal.

listserv

A listserv is fairly primitive (yet still powerful) social networking tool. It is essentially a collection of e-mail addresses linked to one listserv e-mail address. For example, I could create a listserv of all the readers of this book by asking you to send me your e-mail address. (Please feel free to do this, by the way. You can reach me at wkist @kent.edu.)

I could then go through a link on my university's Web page that allows me to create a listserv and name it. Let's say I name the listserv KISTREADERS@LISTSERV .KENT.EDU. Then, as I am the listserv creator, I would go through another link once my listserv is set up and add each person's e-mail address. Any time I want to communicate with these people, I send one e-mail to KISTREADERS@LISTSERV .KENT.EDU, and my message will be received by all the people on my listserv. Listservs can be set up in several configurations with all the people able to send messages to the listserv or with only a few select people allowed to communicate with the group.

Nings

The name "Ning" comes from the Web site Ning.com that provides free networking space for any group of people who want to form an online community. It takes only moments to set up, and then those who want to join the Ning are able to communicate with the other people who have joined that Ning. The Ning looks like a social network environment such as Facebook in that participants create a profile and then post comments and questions to the group. Many educators are using Ning as a safe way of using social networking in the classroom in that it can be set up to be completely private and so that each post to the Ning generates an e-mail to the teacher. Setting up a Ning is free. For a small fee, the Ning creator does have the option of eliminating advertising. There is also an age requirement—children under 13 cannot participate. Please check out the Ning created for readers of this book at: http://sociallynetworkedclassroom.ning.com.

Almost immediately after having done these kinds of community-building activities, I find there is a change in the classroom community. This is most often evident in the comments on the class listserv. Before the advent of Ning.com and other social networking platforms for classrooms, I set up simple listservs in which everyone in the class is a member and all can send messages to each other. The listserv is hosted on my school's server and only requires me to type in the e-mail addresses of each student once, and they are subscribed to the listserv. It is usually after some of these community-building activities that more animated, humorous conversations start on the listserv. After the class was over, Michelle commented on the use of the listserv saying, "The listserv keeps everyone from the class connected through continuously building and maintaining relationships." Ambrosia wrote, "With the listserv, I get several responses to the question (I ask)," and Riley wrote, "It is a very quick and convenient way to contact many people at once, which ultimately saves time." Cindy wrote, "The listserv was great because you knew that there was someone else who was feeling the same anxiety as you just an e-mail away!"

Beyond the listserv, the students begin to share inside jokes in class as well. They begin to circulate sign-up sheets to bring food to class. I've even had two classes design T-shirts commemorating funny lines and events from the class. One student said, "We were always in classes together but never really were a community until now."

QUESTIONS TO CONSIDER

1. What did you have to do successfully as a group member in this activity for the goal to be achieved?
2. What obstacles did you face individually and as a group?
3. How did you overcome these obstacles?
4. What parallels can you draw between this activity and behavior in an online world? What differences are there?

But what does this have to do with literacy? A lot, I would answer, especially in a new media age. Most of us probably still think of writing as a solitary activity. We tend to imagine a lonely writer holed up in an artist's garret, lost in reverie. The reverie part may still be present, but increasingly, writers are collaborating with other writers on texts—writers who may live thousands of miles away.

wikis

Coming from the Hawaiian word for "quick," wikis have become essential for collaborative writing done in an online environment. Anyone can set up his or her own wiki focusing on any topic of choice. There are many platforms available to host wikis such as Wikispaces.com or PBwiki.com. The person who sets up the wiki determines who is allowed to contribute to the wiki. Once those people click on a link on the wiki, they are able to contribute to whatever text is being cocreated there. Some famous examples of wikis are Wikipedia.org and Lostpedia.org.

(Continued)

(Continued)

There are also platforms that simply store a group's commonly used documents, in Word or Excel, for example. GoogleDocs allows for this kind of storage of documents so that colleagues and friends can collaborate on these shared documents from anywhere and at any time.

While in schools we most often still assign writing to be done individually, outside school writing often is done in a collaborative environment such as GoogleDocs or Wikispaces. Texts are shaped collaboratively, drafted by more than one person, and then revised and edited by others—sometimes by hundreds or thousands more people. Wikipedia.org is an example of this; thousands of people across the world actively participate in suggesting and then writing the entries that are never completely finalized. We need to give students practice in working collaboratively to produce these kinds of texts. For several years, I have used a very old reading strategy activity to get at what it means to create a text with a group.

WRITING COLLABORATIVELY

List Group Label With Found Poetry

1. Put students into groups of three or four. Give each group a large piece of chart paper.
2. Tell students that you are going to be giving them a category, such as "birds" or "spiders." Each group member is then going to have a certain amount of time to write down whatever words or phrases come into his or her head related to the category. Each student is to write on one corner or side of the large chart paper.
3. After time is up, each group is to count the total number of words on each chart paper.
4. (Optional) The rest of the original activity suggests that each group then come up with categories in which to group all the words.
5. Direct students to select their "favorite" 10 to 12 words and write them in the center of the chart paper.
6. Students are then directed to take those 10 words and form them into a poem. The teacher may give students the option of adding a certain number of verbs or other modifiers, if so desired.

Source: Adapted from Taba, 1967.

This combined activity takes up to 40 minutes, and for the entire time, students are invariably on task and collaborating with each other. The first part of the activity gets students to compete against other groups in generating words and phrases. The second part of the activity gets students to collaborate in taking some of these words and forming them into a poem. There are occasionally some students who don't do well with this kind of collaborative writing, but there is something about being grouped around a big piece of chart paper that leads to a true collaborative experience as students debate which words should be used to form their poems and then struggle to form these somewhat random words together into a poem. These found poems often stay posted for weeks and are referred to as common reference points for certain groups long after the groups themselves have faded away.

This is an activity that causes the proverbial "light bulb" to go on over the heads of many of my students when we begin to discuss how much writing is done collaboratively today. While students always want to be able to compose individually, they see the advantage to being able to collaborate and how this activity using chart paper can simulate the online writing experience with all its compromise, negotiation, and serendipity.

QUESTIONS TO CONSIDER

1. How do you feel about the poem you collaborated on?
2. Would you have preferred to write a poem individually that used the words?
3. Did it help the poetry writing to have the group brainstorming (listing) activity? Why or why not?
4. List some "rules" or etiquette that needs to apply when writing collaboratively.

Who Is the Audience for Our Writing in a New Media Age?

Not only do we barely know the people we collaboratively write with in this new media age, we may only have a dim notion of who our audience is. This becomes even more complicated when, in a blogging situation, anonymous readers may post comments that run the gamut from cheers to jeers.

AUDIENCE

Snowball Activity

Distribute sheets of standard white copy paper to each student in the room.

1. Direct each student to write his or her name at the top of his or her paper.

(Continued)

(Continued)

2. Direct students to react to a prompt. (It could be anything. The topic of the prompt is irrelevant to the activity.)
3. Have students stand up and, on a signal, wad up their papers into snowballs and throw them across the room.
4. Students should retrieve one snowball from the ground and return to their seats, uncrumple the paper, and react in a sentence or two to what the first person has written.
5. Students should crumple the paper again and then, on a signal, throw the snowball across the room again.
6. Repeat this any number of times.
7. After the last time, ask the student to return the snowball to the original writer (whose name is at the top of the page).

Source: Adapted from Burke, 2000.

blogs and blogging

Blogs are basically online journals or "logs." Over the years, the earlier name (Web log) has been shortened to "blog." There are several free platforms for hosting a blog, giving anyone who wants it a potential instant worldwide audience. A blog can be set up in any number of ways, but the essential components are the entries themselves, which are very similar to page-based diary entries with all of the range of length, style, and content that one would get in any personal journal. What makes blogging a key part of Web 2.0 is their interactive nature. There is usually a link following each entry of a blog for readers to leave comments about the entry. In the past, the only respondent to one's diary entries might be found in the history books. Now, the response could be instantaneous, public, and from a mixture of friends, colleagues, and even strangers.

For years, I've been doing the activity above with students as a kind of story-starter activity and just as an example of an activity that gets kids up and out of their seats and engaging with each other. A few years ago, I was doing this activity and realized that its purposes could broaden to include fostering a dialogue about a principle of literacy in the age of Web 2.0 and, in particular, blogging: How do we think about "audience" in the age of Web 2.0?

Of course, a key objective of writing instruction over the years has been getting kids to think about audience before beginning to write. Audience has implication for everything from language to tone and even to length. We've taught kids to think about audience during every stage of the writing process, even during the prewriting stage when they are brainstorming about what it is they want to say. But what happens during the writing process when the writing we're doing is for an unknown and potentially worldwide audience and a rowdy audience at that, capable of making random comments about what we write?

The breakthrough moment for me was when some students reacted strongly to the comments that had been written on their "snowballs." After the "snowball" has been thrown around the room a few times and commented on by various class members, I ask each student to return his or her snowball to the original writer (whose name is at the top of the page). It was always interesting to see how students voraciously read the comments that others had written on their papers or snowballs. But when the snowball was returned to its original owner, sometimes there were outraged comments, such as "Who wrote this?" or "That's not what I meant. I've been misunderstood!" These comments got me thinking about parallels between the comments on the snowballs and comments that are left on blogs in response to the original entries. I asked the students, "How did it make you feel to get a comment that blatantly disagreed and perhaps even misunderstood what you were saying with your original statement? Would it shape how you wrote your original comment if you knew that you were going to get these comments on what you had written?" This opened up a dialogue around some of the following questions.

QUESTIONS TO CONSIDER

1. How did it make you feel to read comments on your snowball? Did you generally agree with what was written, or was there a comment that you felt was totally "off the wall"? How did that make you feel?
2. How does it change your writing when you don't know who's going to be reading it?
3. Pretend your snowball could fall into the hands of anyone in the world and potentially years later. How would that change what you wrote? How would it change your writing when your audience could be anyone in the world?
4. Does it make you feel any different when you don't know who the commenter is (when the names of the commenter are not required on the snowballs)?
5. In the random reading and writing environment that is Web 2.0, what are some guidelines we should follow when blogging or leaving comments on others' blogs?
6. What are some safeguards that can be built into the blog to prevent malicious or hurtful comments?

How Do We Multitask or Do Things Simultaneously and/or Synchronously?

Being able to perform more than one task simultaneously seems to be a key feature of the new media consumer experience. This is a mixed blessing: people (understandably) rant about drivers who text message behind the wheel, for example. But whether this kind of media multitasking is generally "good" or "bad"—leading to shortened attention spans, perhaps—it seems to be here to stay; people are simultaneously performing tasks that used to be considered mutually exclusive. I have noticed during the writing of this book that I am much more of a multitasker than I have been in the past. During the time I've been writing this paragraph, I've been loading tunes into my iTunes, responding to an e-mail message, and checking my Twitter stream (see Chapter 5). Maybe the paragraph would have been better written if I had been attending to it as a solitary task, but I seem to have fallen into a pattern in which I am more productive if I am multitasking in my digital world. The following activity is an old "outdoor education" game that I have used to simulate what happens when we multitask, perhaps beyond our capacity to perform all tasks effectively.

"THIS IS AN APPLE" ACTIVITY

1. Form a circle with students standing and include yourself (the teacher) in the circle.
2. The teacher is the leader of this game and should be holding two objects that are passable—anything from a couple of key chains to some tennis balls or even some very small stuffed animals.
3. The leader takes one of the objects and passes it to the person on his right and says, "This is an apple." The person must say, "A what?" The leader then responds, "An apple."
4. The person then hands the object to the person on his or her right and says, "This is an apple." The second person must answer, "A what?" The first person turns back to the leader and says, "A what?" The leader says, "An apple." The first person turns to the second person and says, "An apple."
5. The second person turns to the person on his or her right and says, "This is an apple," and the process repeats with the "A what" response coming back down the line to the leader, who responds, "An apple," sending that response all the way back down the line to the person who currently holds the "apple" object.

6. After the "apple" has progressed around the circle about a third of the way, the leader initiates the same pattern to his or her left, turning to the person on his or her left and handing the object, and saying, "This is a banana."

7. The challenge occurs at the point in the circle, usually opposite the leader, when the "apple" and "banana" are passing each other. Participants have to really concentrate to say the correct words and multitask, as they may need to say two different actions and perform two separate tasks at the same time.

This game often leads to quite a range of emotions on the part of the players. Some students can't stop laughing at the way their classmates freeze or mess up when trying to perform tasks simultaneously. Some students genuinely dislike this game for the pressure it puts on them. People either love the challenge of the game, or they have the "deer in the headlights" look as they are forced to concentrate and make sure they are performing the task they need to do in order to keep the objects moving.

If the game breaks down, some students are adamant that we keep playing the game until we get it "right." I've even had groups request to play the game once each class time until they can get the objects going all the way around the circle with no breakdown.

When discussing the issue of multitasking, there are many anecdotes told of roommates who could multitask and roommates who couldn't—of people who can write with music in the background and of people who need absolute silence. We discuss multitasking as a feature of both reading and writing in a new media age. What does it mean when one must attend to different tasks within the overall task of reading? Are people really attending to multiple tasks at the same time or just switching back and forth rapidly? Does this multitasking make a difference to the reader or writer of new media texts?

QUESTIONS TO CONSIDER

1. How did this game make you feel?
2. How is this similar to or different from the kinds of multitasking that people do when working with media tasks?
3. Will people who are not adept at multitasking be able to process media tasks as efficiently as those who can't?
4. There are those who claim that when we multitask, we really aren't attending to more than one task at a time but simply switching rapidly back and forth between different tasks. Do you agree or disagree with this point of view?

How Do New Formats Transform Writing?

People now may be glimpsed writing everywhere, from the baseball game to the food court at the mall, from the jogging trail to the Laundromat. Writing and reading messages from our social networks are permeating almost every moment of our waking lives. While some see this as a positive way to stay connected to friends and family, others see it as intrusive and potentially corrupting to the English language. At the very least, the situation is ripe for discussion, and I have used a well-known poetry-writing activity to focus on the advantages and limitations of such forms as texting and Twitter that demand extremely concise, almost coded writing.

RANDOM PHRASE POEM

1. Give each student a 3 × 5 index card.
2. Direct each student to write a random phrase on the card. The phrase cannot have more than 140 characters.
3. Collect all the students' cards.
4. Read them aloud in random order.
5. Tell the students they have just written a "Random Phrase Poem."

(Note, a variation on this activity is asking students to comment on something they are doing at the moment—as in Twitter—but the drawback to this is that each card then has a variation of "I'm writing on this 3 × 5 card.")

Source: Adapted from Koch, 1970.

QUESTIONS TO CONSIDER

1. Were there any trends or themes in the random phrase poem?
2. How did you feel about the limit of 140 letters?
3. Did you alter something you were going to say based on the length?
4. Apply this experience to the way you communicate outside of school. Has texting altered the way you use the language? If so, how?
5. Has texting made an impact on your writing?

texting

The word *texting* is a shortened way of saying "text messaging"—that is, those very brief messages that are typed into one's cell phone (mobile phone) to communicate with friends and colleagues. Because it is somewhat difficult to type full words using such a small keyboard, many people use abbreviated forms of English words and also emoticons or symbols to communicate their thoughts and ideas.

After doing this activity, students are amused by how funny the random phrase poems are and how amazingly well they hang together, given that they were composed completely randomly. We soon transition into a discussion of what writing affordances such short-form media as Twitter, texting, and social networking allow. At about this time, we read about the novels that are being composed across the world, but mainly in Japan, entirely on cell phones. What is so appealing about this format that causes people to Twitter throughout their own weddings and other major life events? Students seem to be fairly evenly spread across a continuum of those who send thousands of texts a month to those rare students who don't own a cell phone. Our discussion gets quite spirited when we start debating whether text message speak should actually be taught in the English classroom as a form of communication worth being studied.

Pausing to Reflect

After doing many of the activities described above, we take a break and pause to reflect on them. Over several years of getting reactions from my students about these new literacies activities, I've noticed some trends in their comments.

New Spaces for Teaching and Learning

Students like to reflect on the experience of what it's like being a learner in a multiliteracy classroom, especially since my students are going into careers in teaching. Students have said things such as, "These activities allowed more free expression than a typical typed assignment," and "It was a great change of pace from normal classwork, although it was difficult at first to actually figure out what you wanted for us to do." Another student stated, "The important thing to remember is that people love to have choices. These activities are perfect for a person who wants 'choices.'"

These assignments seem to create new spaces for teaching and learning for my students.

One of the key elements of these activities is their engaging nature, bearing out one of the characteristics of new literacies classrooms, that new literacies classrooms are places of student engagement in which students report achieving a "flow" state.

Mindy said, "These activities help keep students interested and having fun learning even in college. We can carry these experiences to our own classrooms."

"I will definitely use activities like this in my classroom someday," Diane predicted. "They allow students to use a more creative outlet of expression that I believe they would enjoy. These lessons give students more variety and keep students thoroughly engaged all of the time."

Sharon made the comment, "New literacy experiences allow students to interact with reading and writing in new ways." Nadine also reflected on the meaning of "literacy": "With the extensive ways to look at what literacy is and how to incorporate it into the classroom, we need to be able to expand our thinking beyond traditional print." I don't know if Nadine and Sharon would have made such comments before taking my class. One can only hope, now that they can "talk the talk," that when they get their own middle school classrooms in less than a year, they will "walk the walk."

The experience of teaching these activities has followed a pattern that has followed me since I was a high school English teacher and was surprised by how the kids reacted to an old silent film. The kids taught me what was important both then and now, and I've tried to follow them (and lead them at the same time). The teaching experiences described in this chapter have taught me that it's not about the technology; there were new literacies when there was no Internet, when there was not even an Apple 2E!

I know that I need to keep on trying to "walk the walk" even as this walk continues to take me places I never anticipated. I also know that I need to be part of a Personal Learning Network (PLN) and get back out there to see what new things visionary teachers are doing. Even if I could not travel physically to Snow Lake as I did in 2003, I could go there again virtually. This time around, as I began to become more active in Web 2.0 myself and to interact via Twitter and various Nings with great educators all over the world, my visits could be ongoing and dialogical and part of the everyday conversations of my life. In the next chapters, we will encounter some of the brave teachers in my PLN as they stare back at their students (and colleagues) and say, "Let's try it!"

A Blog Post From the Field

The biggest drawback is the time and effort it takes to use some of this technology. As a first year teacher, pretty much all of my lesson plans are new lesson plans—it's not like I'm a veteran teacher who is just revamping lessons to put on the Web, so along with trying to find good online resources, I am also trying to plan my units and lessons, period. So obviously technology will take a back burner this year when it comes to planning time. On the flip side, a few of my lessons have been structured around things like podcasts or a wiki Web quest, which has led to some more interesting and active learning lessons. Also, I think using technology helps to validate me as a teacher—it gives me a little bit of street cred, both with the students who are really in tune to the online world and with older teachers, who seem at least mildly impressed that technology can actually work—some of them see it as a weapon that is just going to replace the teacher, but I know I've shown at least one teacher so far that doesn't have to be the case.

Cassie Neumann
English, Theater, and Media Teacher
Brunswick High School
Brunswick, Ohio

3

"Tall"

Social Networking in a Medium-Tech Environment

Many teachers work in districts that have a moderate amount of Internet filtering and blocking. For many of these teachers, one solution may be to set up projects that mimic being on the Web, even if they are not actually connected. Or if they're not mimicking the Internet, these teachers may be online but in a highly protected, fenced-in environment. This chapter provides examples of assignments and assessments that include at least a taste of Web 2.0 at school. First, the issue of staying safe online is addressed with examples of how some educators are dealing with this challenge.

As I began to communicate with educators all over the world and build up my Personal Learning Network (PLN), I quickly saw that the issue that overwhelms any talk of Web 2.0 classroom applications is the issue of keeping our students safe. The decision about whether to take students online and how protected they need to be seems to be a difficult one for educators. Some districts end up becoming locked down with unsupervised surfing strictly prohibited. Other schools find ways to compromise and offer students at least a simulation of what being online is like. Chapter 2 provided some examples of activities that can be done in a situation where there is very little technology available (or as activities to preview and spotlight issues of new literacies). This chapter spotlights educators who are beginning to wade into the shallow waters of a multiliteracies curriculum. For many educators, what prevents them from going deeper (other than their own techno-phobias) is the fear of the dangers that students can find themselves in online.

How Do We Communicate Safely Online?

Most educators feel that the issue of Internet safety must be dealt with somehow before any online activities may occur. Indeed, the overarching issue of Internet safety becomes a "teachable moment," with schools developing or adopting fully written curricula encouraging teachers to bring the lessons of the online world into their classrooms. The Seattle Public Schools, for example, have developed a series of lessons that teachers can use at the middle school level to help kids be safe online. These lessons are grouped around such categories as "Respect and Responsibility," "Cyberbullying: Impacts and Consequences," and "What to Do If You Are Being Cyberbullied." (See the entire curriculum at http://www.seattleschools.org/area/prevention/cbms.html.)

Mike Donlin, Senior Program Consultant, described the genesis of the project:

> My colleague and I began hearing rumblings about what kids were doing on the Internet—initially via e-mail. I began doing some research and got some Internet safety training under my belt. We heard more of the cyberbullying stories. . . . In the meantime, I got connected with the Qwest Foundation, which provided grant money to develop the curriculum. I was able to find a great team, and together, we created the curriculum you see on our Web site.

When I asked him how supportive teachers are of using the curriculum, he responded that the use of the curriculum varies, due to competing demands on time and resources, and that there is no "hammer" to force using it. But one of the compelling reasons for developing the curriculum was a revised school board policy and anti-harassment legislation at the state level that included "electronic means" of bullying, intimidation, and harassment.

SELECTED INTERNET SAFETY CURRICULA

Cybersmart Curriculum (National School Boards Association), http://cybersmart curriculum.org/cyberbullying/nsba/lessons

Digizen, http://www.digizen.org

iMentor Training Network, http://xblock.isafe.org/imtn.php

iSafe, http://www.isafe.org

Media Awareness Network, http://www.media-awareness.ca/english/games/index.cfm

NetSmartz, http://www.netsmartz.org/index.aspx

Sunset Ridge Schools, Northfield, Illinois, http://www.sunsetridge29.net/16661041 4223550860/site/default.asp

Wired Safely, http://www.wiredsafety.org

Other districts deal with the safety issue by investing in a simulated Internet environment. Charlene Entman, Technology Teacher Facilitator/ Webmaster in the Sunset Ridge School District outside of Chicago, reports that their district purchased "Schoolwires," which she describes as a "school-focused content managed system. The product offered several enhancement modules, including blogging, flash photo galleries, podcast hosting, database management, forms, surveys, and search capability." Charlene completed the Anti-Defamation League's (ADL) World of Difference Train-the-Trainer program and became an iSafe certified trainer. She says, "Exposure to both of these programs—along with a growing awareness of online improprieties, copyright concerns, and a naivety among teens, teachers, and parents about the virtues and consequences of electronic communication—caused me to take action and become an advocate of digital citizenship and responsible use of social technology tools." Entman is concerned that adults are not informed about the online world, and she furthermore states, "We need to redefine privacy and develop a model that children can emulate and understand. We need to pressure state governments to include legislation for Internet Safety curriculum guidelines and standards." She sees these steps as allowing educators to "better embrace the Web 2.0 tools and engage the learner in a productive and less compromising way."

Educators who work on developing Web-based educational sites are also very concerned about online safety. Zoey's Room (www.zoeysroom.com) is an afterschool club that launched in 2002 and "meets" online. It is designed to encourage girls to become interested in science, technology, engineering, and math (STEM). As described on their Web site:

> Hip cyber-hostess "Zoey" hosts her own chat room for girls every day after school. She encourages girls to explore STEM topics through fun challenges called Tec-Treks, which expand their knowledge on a range of 21st century skills, including Internet research, databases, word processing, science, business math, digital and video proficiency, robotics, engineering, and Web site design. Additionally, each month, Zoey leads informative chats with "Fab

Female" role models in STEM professions. Currently, Zoey's room administrators are working with partners to disseminate the after school clubs in order to reach members across the nation.

One of the cofounders of Zoey's Room, Erin Reilly, describes how important it was for the site to be safe for participants, even using a third-party vendor to verify any registrant's identification. "Zoey's Room was the first online community geared to youth to pilot test a verification product that checked information against several federal databases, including the National Center for Missing and Exploited Children," says Erin.

Also, within the online community, there are clear rules with sanctions for breaking the rules, including ten-day timeouts. Erin thought that those who had been punished with a timeout would never return to the site, but she's been surprised that they do. "They return because they have a vested interest in the other members they've gotten to know," Erin states, "and because of the creative and fun STEM learning that's happening."

QUESTIONS TO CONSIDER

1. Was there ever a time when you felt unsafe online? Explain what happened and how you resolved the situation.
2. What are some common principles of staying safe online?
3. You've had a chance to look at some of the online safety tutorials. What do you think of them? What are they missing? If you could design an "Internet Safety" tutorial, what would you be sure to include?

What Does "Fair Use" Mean in a Web 2.0 World?

A barrier for many teachers who want to use social networking tools with their students is the fear of plagiarism. Some acknowledge that this kind of thinking is just as outdated as is an old typewriter. Angela Maiers, Independent Literacy Consultant, feels that teachers are stuck in an old paradigm in this regard and tend to get obsessed with who owns knowledge. "It's not only about owning the rights to the content you produce," she says. "It's what you do with it, and how you share it, and what others do with it. I have so many academics say, 'You're giving everything away.' It's no longer my stuff. All my stuff is under Creative Commons Licensing. Creative commons not only means others can use it, but they can also modify it. . . . Under Creative Commons, attribution is always given to the original writer. It turns copyright upside down. In the spirit of 21st century, teachers have to realize that it's not about hoarding."

Still, not all teachers are ready for this paradigm shift and at the very least feel that the characteristics of the Internet provide opportunities for having a dialogue about ownership of ideas. Renee Hobbs (2010), professor at Temple University, has embarked on a project over several years that has led to a clarification of fair use policies for educators. A team of scholars from the Media Education Lab at Temple University; the Program on Information Justice and Intellectual Property at Washington College of Law, American University; and the Center for Social Media, American University, have been studying the issue of fair use in the classroom and have developed a policy statement that can be accessed at http://www.centerforsocialmedia.org/resources/publications/code_for_media_literacy_education.

There are serious implications from this policy for educators who want to use new media in their classrooms, including copyrighted material. The key provision of this policy is that if the educator is repurposing (transforming) the original work, then that constitutes fair use. Students also are under the constraint of demonstrating how the copyrighted material has been repurposed in whatever text they are creating. Obviously, this is a thorny issue for teachers, and the issue of fear of plagiarism is often mentioned as a reason teachers give for limiting new media applications in the classroom. Still, at the very least, there are some real opportunities for dialogue with students about what is and what is not fair use. Surely, this distinction will need to be made by the student once he or she enters the "real world," so isn't this a conversation we should have with our kids in school?

QUESTIONS TO CONSIDER

1. Have you ever plagiarized? You don't need to give the specifics, but what led you to that point?
2. Does having read the policy statement from the Center for Social Media help make more clear the fair use issue for both students and teachers? If not, what still confuses you?
3. Some have the opinion that in a Web 2.0 world, every text belongs to everybody and that anyone should be able to use texts created by others to form new hybrid texts, whether for educational use or not. Do you agree or disagree with this opinion, and why or why not?

What Does It Mean to Have a Dialogue With a Text Using Hyperlinks?

I like students to practice having a dialogue with a text by having them e-mail me their responses to the text in the form of double-entry journals with some embedded hyperlinks. Double-entry journals have been used by teachers for years to promote active reading. There are many formats to double-entry journals, but most involve having the student copy an interesting quote from a text, and then, either on the other side of the page or below, comment on that quote (hence the term *double entry*). Suggesting that students submit these journals electronically with some hyperlinks thrown in simply updates this assignment for a screen-based literacy world. This practice also supports a characteristic of new literacies classrooms, that there are think-alouds by the teacher who model working through problems using certain symbol systems—a double-entry journal can be used as a kind of think-aloud not only as a student "reads" and reacts to any number of texts but also as he or she is creating in these different media, so that the double-entry journal becomes a kind of running record of the artist's process.

hyperlink

A hyperlink is the gateway that allows the reader to go to a different site by simply clicking on it. This link can be highlighted in a different color or the reader may have to guess which sign on the page is a hyperlink by holding the cursor over the sign. The embedded hyperlinks form the interactive nature of the Web, making reading any Web-based text like reading the old "Choose Your Own Adventure" books in which the reader could construct the narrative in any way he or she pleased.

Before turning kids loose on this assignment, it makes sense to do such a think-aloud, modeling for the students how one has a dialogue with a text, by annotating, forming questions and opinions, and thinking of possible connections (which become the hyperlinks) while reading. The teacher can also go further and demonstrate the think-aloud while composing the double-entry journal itself, thus modeling the thoughts that go through one's head during the composing process.

Such an "old school" activity as Double-Entry Journaling gives students practice at what it means to have a dialogue with a text (no matter what that text is), and another advantage of assigning double-entry journals is that they are difficult to plagiarize in that the student is giving his or her personal reaction to a very specific section of the text.

HYPERLINKED DOUBLE-ENTRY JOURNALS

Nine times during the semester, you will have the opportunity to turn in a double-entry journal. These journals will be in response to the required texts, articles provided by Dr. Kist, your literature circle book, and other texts.

You will turn these journals in via e-mail. Each Weblog log should include three quotes that have moved you in some way from the assigned readings. You should copy the quote from the text, note the page number, and then state in a paragraph why you have selected this quote. You will be evaluated based on how thoroughly you explain your reaction to each quote. You will also need to embed two hyperlinks per journal, linking some word or phrase to either another Word document you have created or a Web site.

You will be held to a standard for each of these journals according to the following criteria:

1. Are you reacting to three quotes (including page numbers) from the texts? What was it about the quote that you found interesting? Is there something about the quote with which you passionately disagree? Does the quote confuse you in some way? (5 points)
2. Are you suggesting specific implications for your future practice as a classroom teacher of adolescents? How will the quote help your practice when you are a teacher? (5 points)
3. What is your personal reaction overall to these readings—likes, dislikes, epiphanies? (5 points)
4. Have you included two hyperlinks related to what you have read? (5 points)

"After I learned how to annotate, I wanted to annotate everything. It was really fun. . . . It took just as much time, but it wasn't as boring as writing a paper about what we were doing." —Andrea

Students appreciate being able to generate a genuine dialogue with a text, but the most often-heard reaction to this assignment is how "addicting" it is to write with hyperlinks—the same word that students used in relation to writing the multigenre autobiographies in Chapter 2. Writing with included hyperlinks even became "addicting" to some students who hadn't ever written for a screen-based text. Some students would take a text, such as a ♭, and embed hyperlinks throughout the text that would lead to definitions, elaborations, or explanations of the author's intent. Students quickly got the hang of writing in a nonlinear format (see Chapter 2).

QUESTIONS TO CONSIDER

1. What did you think of doing this assignment? Did you see it as worthwhile? Why or why not?
2. What happens to the reading experience when you start "talking back" to the text you are reading? Does it change your perception of the text itself? Of the author? Of the ideas expressed in the text?
3. How is making a double-entry journal similar to and/or different than a think-aloud that a composer does when creating a text?

Still, this double-entry journal activity is fairly one-sided, with students e-mailing me their double-entry journals and awaiting a response from me. To more fully approximate the interactivity of a Web 2.0 experience, many teachers are moving toward incorporating a blog, even if it is completely unavailable to the outside world, as a kind of home base for each student, providing a platform for his or her own response.

What Are the Generally Accepted Rules for Blogging?

Many teachers ease into using Web 2.0 by first creating blogs within a completely closed school network, operating as a kind of "Intranet." The protected environment of such an Intranet allows the teacher to monitor content and step in when there are situations that demand some kind of intervention. It actually makes a lot of sense to talk about the principles of blogging without being online. Students can create profiles that link directly to their blogs, just as one would in a truly online environment. There are several different protected environments for hosting student blogs.

Intranet

An Intranet can do anything that the Internet can do, except it is completely protected and cut off from the real Internet. By setting up a fake Internet, an organization can have all the benefits of social networking but only with people who belong to that organization. This kind of protected environment can also essentially be set up online through use of Ning.com or Moodle.com—environments that can be completely sealed off and protected from outside members.

Heidi Whitus, English and communication teacher at Communications Arts High School in San Antonio, Texas, hosts her high school students' blogs on Turnitin.com and Moodle but goes to the Internet site Blogspot for her college students. She would use Blogspot for her high school students, but it is blocked at her school. "I wouldn't advise signing up for Turnitin solely for the discussion function," she says. "It's too expensive. But since our school had the account anyway, we're trying to use it in as many ways as we can."

SELECTED PROTECTED SITES FOR HOSTING BLOGS

http://www.epals.com

http://www.turnitin.com

http://socialmediaclassroom.com

http://edublogs.org/campus

http://www.21classes.com

http://moodle.org

http://classblogmeister.com

http://drupal.org

Often teachers will introduce blogging to their students by teaching the routines and conventions of blogging, feeling that the key to a successful experience, whether offline or online, is setting up the agreed upon group norms at the beginning of the process. This is similar to Nancie Atwell's description of how one begins the year by doing minilessons on procedures surrounding a reader or writer workshop (Atwell, 1998).

William Chamberlain, fifth-grade teacher in Noel, Missouri, writes that his students, their parents, and the community have been very respectful of the ground rules he has set up for blogging. They are as follows:

1. It is okay to be critical, but it is not okay to be mean.
2. If you have something negative to say, combine it with something positive.
3. Make sure your comment stays on the topic.
4. If you don't have anything to write, don't write anything.
5. Always remember that they can comment on your post, too!

Chamberlain relates that it was a simple process to write a letter home about the use of a class blog, and that he encounters surprisingly little resistance. Chamberlain reports that once he explains that the blog will be moderated, he has had no parent complaints. "I've had contact with people from other school districts that are amazed that I'm allowed to do what I do," he reports.

Staying safe online is part of introducing blogging into the classroom for many teachers. George Mayo, seventh-grade teacher in Montgomery

"I tell my students that what they write will be accessible by people around the world and that once it is published, it will always be accessible." —William Chamberlain

County Schools in Maryland, begins the year with an open discussion of ways to stay safe on the Web. He starts by showing the students a video that he found on YouTube (http://mrmayo.wordpress.com/2008/09/28/staying-safe-online) and has them discuss what "dumb things" the girl in the video is doing, such as posting her home address and phone number online or linking to pictures of her friend in a bathing suit. George arranged for students from a different school to watch the same video, and as the blogging began, the students from each school read the students' posts from the other school and commented back and forth. This was followed by a live Skype video conference about it all. Students were also expected to initiate several blog posts on the subject of Internet safety. Most teachers have extensive discussions with their students about online safety and etiquette, especially if they are going to be posting anything on the open, unfiltered Web (which will be discussed more in the next chapter).

Some teachers just want to give their students practice using these Web 2.0 tools, so many of these assignments simply serve as introductions to the medium of blogging. Rachelle Ring, sixth-grade teacher at West Branch Elementary in West Branch, Ohio, and one of my former students, has taken advantage of an Intranet setup in her school and has set up blogs for all her students. She monitors all student blog comments and admits that she has trouble keeping up. "It's difficult when I need to get around the room to answer questions or supervise students who may be off task," she says. However, Rachelle feels it is worth the trouble; she has noticed quite a jump in student engagement with writing as she has added blogging to her classroom. She plans to add online literature circles with another teacher in the building and have students collaborate and communicate about the literature they are reading through blogging rather than traditional classroom writing.

"This is their media. . . . I believe students are interested in reading and writing because of this tool." —Rachelle Ring

BLOGGING INTRODUCTORY ASSIGNMENT

Rachelle Ring
West Branch Elementary
West Branch, Ohio
mcspace.mcesc.k12.oh.us/ring/

Creating avatars: http://www.moeruavatar.com/index_en.shtml

After you create your avatar, save it as a picture.

Next, you will need to upload it to your page.

1. Log on.
2. Click on your profile (in gray).
3. Click on "Change Site Picture."
4. Scroll down and click "Browse." (Find the picture you saved and click on it.)
5. Scroll to bottom of page and click "Upload New Icon."

Rubric for Blogging Entries

5 points

Original thought that answers question

Supported by example or quote from the book

Minimum of 50 words

3 points

Contains two of the three elements listed above

1 point

Contains one of the three elements listed above

0 points

No entry

*To see Mrs. Ring's blog entry, click on "Mrs. Ring" on the right side of the page. Then click "Personal Blog."

To respond, click on your blog in gray bar at top of page.

Next, click "Post a New Entry."

Scroll down and hit "Post" when complete.

Heidi Whitus starts her semester with a blogging exercise (see Table 3.1) that gets kids interacting with various media texts at the same time she is giving them practice with blogging. Heidi feels that the quality of the discussions is better when the blogging system is in place—that the discussion online is more spontaneous, with greater parity

"I like the fact that students can see how easy it is for anybody to 'publish' now, so they will be more critical of the information they see on the Internet." —Heidi Whitus

Table 3.1 Early Blog Assignment

		Advanced	*Proficient*	*Partially Proficient*	*Not Proficient*
Activity 1	1. Listen to the podcast of "On the Media" at least twice during the semester. You can subscribe to it from iTunes or go to http://www.onthemedia.org. Summarize the stories you heard on your blog. Be sure to make a note of the dates of the podcasts you listened to.	• More than two shows listened to • Detailed summaries and reflections of both stories • Dates included	• Two or more shows listened to • Summaries of both stories • Dates included	• Two or more shows listened to • Insufficient summaries of stories • Dates not included	• Two or more shows listened to • No summaries of stories • Dates not included
Activity 2	2. Read the San Antonio *Express-News* and a newspaper from another city on at least three different days. Compare the types of stories covered, the amount of advertising, and the kinds of feature stories ("soft" news) in the two papers.	• Read papers on more than three days • Detailed comparison and reflections of both papers	• Read papers on three days • Comparison of both papers	• Read papers on fewer than three days • Slight comparison of both papers	• Read papers on fewer than two days • No comparison of papers

		Advanced	*Proficient*	*Partially Proficient*	*Not Proficient*
Activity 3	3. Watch television news from at least three different channels (WOAI, KENS-5, KSAT, PBS, KABB are the local stations, and if you have cable you should also include CNN, FOXNews, and/or MSNBC); *compare* their approach to broadcast journalism by choosing a specific story and describing the differences in how the different channels cover the story.	• Watched more than three channels • Detailed comparison and reflections of all stories	• Watched three channels • Comparison of all stories	• Watched fewer than three channels • Slight comparison of stories	• Watched fewer than two channels • No comparison of stories
Activity 4	4. Watch at least two of the following movies about mass media outside of class, and summarize the films and your reflections of them in your blog: • *All the President's Men* • *Broadcast News* • *The China Syndrome* • *Shattered Glass* • *Network* • *Good Night and Good Luck* • *His Girl Friday* • *Citizen Kane*	• Watched more than two films • Detailed summaries of all films	• Watched two films • Summaries of both films	• Watched two films • Slight summaries of film	• Watched fewer than two films • No summaries of films

among the students: "Everyone must participate, and nobody can monopolize the discussion." She also uses the Discussion Board feature in Turnitin, but finds it is more suited for targeted prompts when all students are responding to the same prompt within a limited time frame.

Hearing about what these teachers were doing inspired me, so over the past year, I have begun to set up blogs with my own students. The following is a rubric that I developed for an assignment that involves students' blogging inside a protected environment while I monitor comments from all students.

BLOG CRITERIA

At Least Four Blog Entries (10 points)

Is each entry at least two paragraphs in length?

Are the entries spread out throughout the semester or clustered at the due date?

Reflection of Course Content or Application in the Entries (30 points)

Are there multiple references to course experiences?

Texts and articles read

Class activities and discussion

Field trip

Other reading and writing life experiences

Are you reacting to specific quotes (include page numbers or link) from the texts? What was it about the quote that you found interesting? Is there something about the quote with which you passionately disagree? Does the quote confuse you in some way?

Are there attempts to integrate multiple viewpoints, weaving in both class readings and other participants' postings into the discussion of the subject?

Are there attempts to apply what has been learned in class to your upcoming student teaching and beyond? Are you suggesting specific implications for your future practice as a classroom teacher of adolescents?

Are your ideas explained in such a way that they are understandable?

Responses to Other's Blog Entries (20 points)

Are you responding to other students' blogs?

Is there some evidence that you are responding to blogs outside the class?

Are the responses thoughtful or shallow? (Example of shallow: "You da man!" or "I agree" without elaborating)

Evidence of Pleasure "Reading" (20 points)

Is there evidence that you have been encountering a wide variety of texts for fun? (These could include mentions of attending films, watching television, playing video games, going to music concerts or other live events such as plays, surfing the Web, reading books, reading graphic novels, or going to an art gallery or poetry reading, to name a few examples.)

Multimedia in the Entries (10 points)

Do some of your blog entries include not only text but also some other media?

Links to Web sites

Links to YouTube clips

Links to wikis

Links to sound files

Other

Mechanics (10 points)

Are there typos and/or mistakes in the writing?

(Note: Some alternative spellings that are obviously "Text Speak" are allowed.)

The most common response I get from students, after blogging for a few weeks, is that they had not previously thought of it as a useful teaching and learning activity. Students mention that they are very familiar with blogs that are set up to show off family pictures or to sound off about some political issue. But they haven't seen blogs used as a platform for learning, as a way to reflect about what they're learning in a public way, and in a way that allows for feedback not only from the teacher but also from their classroom peers. Students take pride in their blogs in a way that they would never show off a typical homework assignment that shuttles its way back-and-forth between the teacher and the student. With a blog as a homework assignment, they can potentially have a worldwide audience if they decide to share the URL with an audience.

QUESTIONS TO CONSIDER

1. How does keeping a blog help improve your learning (or not improve it)?
2. Have you encountered someone who has not followed blogging etiquette? Explain the situation and how you handled it.
3. What are some of the differences between a blog you might publish for family and friends and a blog that you publish to document your learning and thinking? What are some of the similarities between those two general types of blogs?

How Do We Co-construct What We're Reading and Studying?

Many teachers talk to their students about how a blog—or any form of social networking—needs to be more than just a place to pontificate. As literacy consultant Angela Maiers says, "I teach students that you have to have a plan of engagement and these questions help: What is my purpose? What is my outcome? What is my contribution and my responsibility? What do I expect from my audience?" Maiers advocates that 70% of what one posts be sharing resources or providing links rather than lecturing or giving online speeches. "This is purposeful, mindful literacy," she says.

Literature Circles on Blogs

To bring about some of the give-and-take dialogue that Maiers is talking about, some teachers decide to transition existing classroom literature circles into an online environment. Teachers are attempting to replicate the face-to-face literature circle experience in several ways. Using a blog format and setting it up so that it is protected from the public is one way of allowing students to discuss what they're reading in an online environment that is completely for the eyes of the class only. Rachelle Ring decided to set up her literature circles as part of her classroom blogging. She designed a rubric to assess the students' blog activities (Table 3.2).

Literature Circles on Wikis

Another way of simulating the literature circle experience online is to set up a wiki and ask students to contribute their ideas to it. As mentioned earlier, a "wiki" is a text that is collaboratively written online. The most famous example of a wiki is Wikipedia (http://www.wikipedia.com). I created a wiki (using pbwiki.com) for my students who are future English teachers. I challenged them to find teaching ideas related to the literary canon so that they could build together the background knowledge and pedagogy strategies they would need to teach these great works.

Table 3.2 Rubric for Blogging Responses to a Novel

Mrs. Ring's Class

	Number of Entries	*Class Participation*	*Reflection*	*Writing*
Superb! Stellar! Wow! 10 points	Ten blog entries are made. At least five must be in response to other postings. All entries are reflective and detailed.	Responses make reference to questions and comments raised during reading and class activities.	Text-self, text-text, and text-world connections are made throughout responses. At least two of each. Total of six.	All responses are clear, concise, and coherent.
Good 8–9 points	Nine blog entries are made. At least four are made in response to other postings. Most entries are reflective and detailed.	Most responses make reference to questions and comments raised during reading and class activities.	Text-self, text-text, and text-world connections are made throughout responses. Total of four to five.	Most responses are clear, concise, and coherent.
Satisfactory 7 points	Eight entries are made. At least three are made in response to other entries. Some entries are reflective and detailed.	Some responses make reference to questions and comments raised during reading and class activities.	Text-self, text-text, and text-world connections are made throughout responses. Total of three.	Some responses are clear, concise, and coherent.
Needs improvement 6 points	Seven or fewer entries are made. Two or fewer are in response to other postings. Most entries are not reflective and detailed.	Less than half of responses make reference to questions and comments raised during reading and class activities.	Text-self, text-text, and text-world connections are made throughout responses. Two or fewer.	Most responses are not clear, concise, and coherent.

CANONICAL TEXT WIKI

You will be assigned a canonical text at random. Throughout the semester, you will be expected to collect 20 instructional strategy and/or assessment ideas that could be used in the teaching of this canonical text. These strategies should include a variety of traditional and alternative strategies (that are all supported by the standards). You will post these ideas on a wiki that is located at _____ pbworks.com. Your challenge is to find as many useful ideas as possible. In April, you will show off your wiki page to the class and discuss the different strategies you have created. You may work together on a wiki page.

Critique Sheet: Canonical Text Wiki Name ____________________

Variety of Ideas (30 points)

Do the ideas involve a variety of tasks, a variety of media (not just print)?

Do the ideas include some pre-reading, during-reading, and post-reading activities?

Do the ideas include a variety of group and individual activities?

Are the ideas creative? (Not just online worksheets)

20 Ideas (10 points)

Are 20 separate ideas represented?

Position of Reader (10 points)

Do the ideas encourage the reader to make choices and be critical readers (rather than emphasizing the "correct" idea)?

Do the ideas engage the student in a creative way?

Usability of Ideas (10 points)

Are the ideas doable in most typical school settings?

Standards Based (10 points)

Are the ideas able to be aligned with the Ohio standards?

(Note: It is not necessary to list indicators for each idea.)

Clarity of the Ideas (10 points)

Are the ideas explained in such a way that they are understandable?

Are the ideas thoroughly explained? (Not just a link to a lesson plan)

Citations (10 points)

If the ideas aren't original, are they cited with a functioning link or other citation? (Each idea needs to be cited.)

Mechanics (10 points)

Are there typos and/or mistakes in the writing? (Note: This does not include mistakes that may be the fault of the technology.)

Web site can be navigated.

Font is large enough, readable.

Ironically, I've noticed that students tend to get somewhat competitive with this assignment, which is supposed to teach them to collaborate. Students seem to relish contributing the most original YouTube video, for example, or decorating their spaces with the most interesting graphics. It all makes for a very interesting wiki to read and one that continues to grow and develop throughout the course, so that a rubric almost becomes superfluous; the wiki begins to morph and strains the boundaries of the preset rubric.

QUESTIONS TO CONSIDER

1. How does it change your reading experience when you are responding with other readers of the same text? Does it take away from the experience or enrich it?
2. What is it like cocreating a text, as you did with the wiki project, with someone else? What would you do differently the next time you try to collaborate on a text? What would you do in the same way?

How Can We Create Portfolios to Look at Work Over a Period of Time?

As mentioned in Chapter 2, a wiki can also be set up for each student as a kind of interactive portfolio system (and essentially a Web site), with students uploading examples of their work throughout an entire year. After a student badgered me to allow their portfolios to be put online, I took my Reading Portfolio and Writing Portfolio assignments that I used to collect on paper and shifted them to an online environment using a wiki. Not only can the teacher and student see a progression of work over a semester or year but also the other students can comment on the work of their classmates if the portfolios are established from the beginning as open to be shared. I usually set up one class wiki and then link to a separate page for each of my students. For now, the assignment is still traditional enough that it is set up to revolve around the reading and writing of page-based texts (although students have the freedom to respond to the texts in a multimodal fashion).

ONLINE READING PORTFOLIO

You should read a book (of your choice) for at least two hours a week. This should be "pleasure" reading, not readings for one of your classes. Now is the time to read books that you have always wanted to read but haven't had a chance. This reading should be fun, so if something you start is tedious, please abandon it and choose something that is not a chore for you to pick up.

Responses to what you are reading will be sent to Dr. Kist via e-mail twice per semester.

The following expectations for your reading portfolio should be uploaded to the class wiki.

1. Two e-mail exchanges with Dr. Kist. Copy and paste both your message and Dr. Kist's response into a Word document. It is your responsibility to save these e-mail messages! You will be graded on whether you have sent in your e-mails on time and whether you have turned in all e-mails sent by Dr. Kist (including late reminders). Please put the e-mails in chronological order. (20 points)
2. A list of your reading territories. You will turn in a list of your territories as a reader using Atwell, 1998, pp. 134–135, as a guide. You will be graded on quality, not quantity (please don't make things up!). Take some time with this list. Don't just generate it at the last minute. Build on the list you turned in as part of your literacy autobiography. (15 points)
3. Your multigenre literacy autobiography. (5 points)
4. Your Reading Record Form. (20 points)
    - Try new authors, subjects, purposes, and genres; expand your reading schemas. Keep track of what you are reading using the Reading Record Form (see Atwell, 1998, Appendix G, p. 498).
    - Read for pleasure for at least two hours a week.
    - Assigned texts for this or any other course are not permitted as pleasure reading.
5. A collection of poetry and song lyrics that have moved you in your reading.
6. A collection of multimedia texts that have helped to shape you.
7. A reflective letter to Dr. Kist describing what this assignment has meant to you. Have you grown as a reader? If not, why not? What now? What are some goals you have for your reading in the future? Can you see any benefits of such an assignment for middle school and high school English and language arts students? (20 points)

Source: Adapted from Atwell, 1998.

ONLINE WRITING PORTFOLIO

You will be evaluated based on your attempt to challenge yourself as a writer. Your writing portfolios will be graded on how thoroughly you meet these expectations. You will upload the following to the class wiki:

1. Writing Goal (originally sent via e-mail): "What is a writing goal I have for myself this fall? What is something that I have always wanted to write?" You will be graded on whether you have sent in your e-mail message on time and whether you have turned in all e-mails sent by Dr. Kist (including late reminders). (10 points)

   Try to write about something that really matters to you. Perhaps you'd like to attempt some new topics, purposes, audiences, genres, forms, or techniques.

2. A list of your Writing Territories: You will turn in a list of your territories as a writer using Atwell, 1998, pp. 121–122, as a guide. You will be graded on how specific you are—notice that Atwell doesn't just say, "My students," for example. She fleshes this out by saying, "What they do and what it means." Take some time with this list. Don't just generate it at the last minute. Build on the list you turned in as part of your literacy autobiography. (10 points)

3. Element(s) of your multigenre literacy autobiography that deals with writing (if any). (Optional)

4. Copy of the "Peer Writing Conference Record" (Atwell, 1998, p. 505) that you filled out in class with your partner. (5 points)

5. Reaction to the response you got from your partner (one paragraph). How did this response make you feel? Did you incorporate any suggestions from your partner in your finished work, or did you ignore his or her suggestions? (5 points)

6. Turn in the final draft of the piece as well as all drafts. You need to have at least two rough drafts in addition to your final draft.

   Make sure you include all drafts. You will be graded on whether you provide evidence of a progression of work (at least two rough drafts plus a final draft). If you try to write different things (which is to be encouraged!) turn in drafts of things you abandon. (5 points)

   Check for mechanics errors. (5 points)

(Continued)

(Continued)

Does the work meet the personal writing goal or desire you've set for yourself? (It's OK if you have changed your goal through the writing as long as you document that change.) (10 points)

7. Turn in an editing checksheet (Atwell, 1998, p. 506) of mistakes you typically make when you write. You can use this list to check your writing against whenever you edit and proofread. This list can be accumulated from "mistakes" you notice in your writing for any course you are taking or in any situation. (5 points)
8. Enter words you don't know how to spell or aren't certain of on the personal spelling list you keep in your spelling folder. (See Atwell, 1998, Appendix H, p. 501.) This list can be accumulated from "mistakes" you notice in your writing for any course you are taking or in any situation. (5 points)
9. (Optional) Please feel free to include one or more pieces of writing from another class and/or something that you've written that has been published and/or just something that you've written of which you are proud.
10. A one-page reflective letter to Dr. Kist describing what this assignment has meant to you. Have you grown as a writer? If not, why not? What now? What are some goals you have for your writing in the future? Can you see any benefits of such an assignment for middle school and high school English and language arts students? (10 points)

Source: Adapted from Atwell, 1998.

QUESTIONS TO CONSIDER

1. If you have ever kept a portfolio before, think about the differences between that portfolio and the portfolio you kept online. How did having your portfolio online improve the experience? How did it lessen the experience?
2. Did knowing that classmates would be viewing your portfolio shape how you constructed the portfolio? Did the public nature of the portfolio make you censor yourself in any way?
3. What surprised you about comments people made on your portfolio? Were these comments helpful or not to your growth as a reader and/or writer?

By carefully testing the waters in a protected space, teachers can provide the element of social networking they want for their students while getting a chance to practice online etiquette, format, and expression. Some of these teachers decide after this time in the "baby pool" to attempt to go into the "deep end." These explorations will be described in Chapter 4.

A Blog Post From the Field

In December of 2006, I set up my blog. At first, I used the blog to communicate with my students. I would ask questions and get some responses. Sometimes, I just used it for fun stuff.

In the spring semester of 2008, my homeroom finally got to work on their own blogs. But I really wanted all my students to be able to create posts and get comments instead of just my homeroom. I also decided that creating 60+ blogs for them to work on was way too much work. So now I am busy setting them up as coauthors on a blog so that they all will publish on one blog. This will save me tons of set up and monitoring time. It will also help me minimize the amount of time my students are changing their themes or adding widgets to their blogs.

This summer, I attended NECC in San Antonio and was amazed by the number of people, but I wasn't surprised by what they were using. I discovered the Classroom 2.0 Ning and started using Twitter. Both of these sites really helped me find new and innovative tools to use. I have experimented with many different tools to see what can be useful to me and to my class. I also use an RSS feed through Bloglines to keep track of the posts of my favorite education bloggers.

One example of a great tool I found from another online educator was Voicethread. Voicethread allows narration of pictures or video with the addition that other people can also comment on the Voicethread. I incorporated it into a science assignment at the end of last year.

William Chamberlain
Fifth-Grade Teacher
Noel Elementary
Noel, Missouri

4

"Grande"

Social Networking in a High-Tech Environment

> An increasing number of teachers are in schools that allow students to have unfiltered access to such sites as Blogger, YouTube, Ning, and PBWiki.com. These teachers are able to more fully realize the learning opportunities that Web 2.0 applications afford. This chapter includes ideas for how to structure assignments in schools that allow for some Internet surfing that is less restricted.

What Is It Like Being Part of the Blogosphere?

Chapter 3 focused on classrooms in which the students and teachers participate in a kind of offline-online world hybrid. Most of the teachers I talked to wished they could teach in a freer environment, their idea being that one doesn't learn to drive by watching movies about driving. But an increasing number of teachers actually are getting access to a less-filtered Internet experience, and the assignments they develop prove to be quite tantalizing to the teachers and classrooms that remain more quarantined.

If a discussion of online etiquette is needed in an Intranet situation, most anyone would agree that learning wise consumerism of the Web 2.0 is even more necessary when kids are allowed a little more unfiltered access. Interestingly, several teachers interviewed for this chapter mentioned that a crucial first step in helping students negotiate the Web is for the teachers first to become part of the world of Web 2.0 themselves. Just by reading some blogs and participating in some Nings, teachers can pick up many ideas as well as pick up the knack of navigating this new landscape themselves.

"I see Twitter as kind of a teacher's lounge on the Internet. It is a place where I can ask a question and get an answer." —William Chamberlain

"Actually, I started down this road myself first. My professional blog, Remote Access, started before my classroom blogs. I decided that I needed a place and a voice. Only after I was comfortable working this way did I bring my kids into it. Now, looking back, I realize I was slow moving and very careful, worried about many things that I didn't need to be." —Clarence Fisher

William Chamberlain has joined the Classroom 2.0 Ning (http://www.classroom20.com) and the Fireside Learning Ning (http://firesidelearning.ning.com). He explains that Fireside Learning is a much smaller Ning and that he is more active there. "I enjoy it because of the diversity of the members," he says. "It isn't the same type of conversation as on 2.0. I think that smaller groups fit my needs better, but I tend to do much more reading than discussion. Sometimes it is because of my lack of time, and sometimes it is because I don't have anything to add. I do enjoy reading what other people are thinking, though. It helps stretch me." Chamberlain is also active on Twitter, which is how I met him.

Once teachers have been an active part of the blogosphere themselves, they want to bring their students along. Teachers who teach in schools with minimal filters will sometimes test the waters just by having students check in (or subscribe) to several preselected blogs written by people out in the world. The teachers usually have expectations that students must visit a certain number of blogs per week, make a certain number of comments on those blogs, and then make at least one blog entry once they have their own blogs. Some teachers mandate that students set up subscriptions to certain blogs, which they can do using such platforms as Google Reader (accessed via Google.com), which allows you to subscribe to any number of blogs so that you will receive the most recent post from that blog (so that you don't have to go to the blog itself for each new post; it will come to your reader). Teachers may also use the blogging search engine Technorati.com to show students how to search for key topics mentioned in blogs across the world. Technorati is a search engine for blog content, so that by typing in a search term, one is able to find all the blog entries in which that search term has been used.

Before turning students loose into the wide open blogosphere, however, the teachers I interviewed talk again about guidelines for blogging, perhaps with a different spin than was described in a previous chapter. This time, there is not only a reminder about net etiquette (sometimes called "netiquette") but also some acknowledgment that the students will be interacting with and leaving comments on the blogs of strangers, those outside the classroom community. Indeed, these students are about to become part of the community of bloggers that is international, and that's really the point of blogging!

Clarence Fisher, of Joseph H. Kerr School in Snow Lake Manitoba, makes sure that his students understand and follow the "Blogging Guidelines," which were originally written by Bud Hunt (http://budtheteacher.com) with his blogging students and redacted by Darren Kuropatwa (http://adifference.blogspot.com).

BUD HUNT'S BLOGGING GUIDELINES

1. Students using blogs are expected to treat blogspaces as classroom spaces. Speech that is inappropriate for class is not appropriate for your blog. While I encourage you to engage in debate and conversation with other bloggers, we also expect that you will conduct yourself in a way that would be acceptable in the classroom.

2. Never *ever ever* give out or record personal information on your blog. Your blog is a public space on the Internet. Don't share anything that you don't want the world to know. For your safety, be careful what you say too. Don't give out your phone number or home address. This is particularly important to remember if you have a personal online journal or blog elsewhere.

3. Again, your blog is a public space. And if you put it on the Internet, odds are really good that it will stay on the Internet. Always. That means ten years from now when you are looking for a job, it might be possible for an employer to discover some really hateful and immature things you said when you were younger and more prone to foolish things. Be sure that anything you write you are proud of. It can come back to haunt you if you don't.

4. Never link to something you haven't read. While it isn't your job to police the Internet, when you link to something, you should make sure it is something that you really want to be associated with. If a link contains material that might be creepy or make some people uncomfortable, you should probably try a different source.

Once students begin to master the logistics of blogging and are becoming part of an interactive blogging community, the teachers will often get to a "Now what?" stage. How can the format and medium of blogging be used for teaching and learning purposes?

Clarence selects certain blogs that support his curriculum and expects students to read and comment on them in a systematic way.

BLOGOSPHERE TASKS

1. Direct students to make their own blogs and get Google accounts (Google Reader, iGoogle, and Google Docs).

2. Provide students with some blogs to start viewing such as Nata Village, Dvice, Afrigadget, and Jan Chipchase's Future Perfect. This is on an iGoogle tab that is shared with students.

3. Direct students to go to Global Voices Online and choose a feed from one country (other than the United States or Canada) and one topic such as health, photography, or history.

4. Direct students to find a few (usually not more than 6–8) student bloggers to subscribe to. Be careful to limit the number of student bloggers, or else it can get overwhelming.

5. From these blogs, they must write or podcast one thing per week that is important to them, to society, that catches them somewhere somehow. About once a month, conference with each student about whom they are reading, what they are learning, what they are getting, and what they need.

6. Also, once a week, have a class in which they can only leave comments for people. Comments are very important as they develop a sense of community inside of the class. They also must record all of the comments they leave for others on a Google spreadsheet so that over time we can track these, the number, quality of them, and so on. This gives us a way to discuss good commenting skills.

7. When studying a specific unit—for example, environmental issues—find a few blogs that are good sources of information for kids to follow. Make a new iGoogle tab and share this with the class. Then direct students to spend a day or two searching for more blogs that they like on this issue and write a blog post recommending two or three more to their classmates with full reasons why. Then spend some time reading these posts and exploring these blogs, and then out of all of these recommendations, vote and choose another two or three that as a class they want to read. This brings us to about six total. After that, if the blogs they had recommended didn't make it onto the class required reading list, they are free to add the others they had found (or which had been found by others) to their own tab. This way, they have my list, a class-chosen list, and some of their own personal choices as well.

—Clarence Fisher

QUESTIONS TO CONSIDER

1. What are the advantages to being part of the blogosphere rather than blogging in a more protected environment? What are the pitfalls of being part of the blogosphere?
2. What is something that surprised you about what you encountered on someone's blog? What did you learn from the blogs you read?
3. If you made a comment on someone's blog from outside the classroom, what motivated you to choose that blog entry to comment on? Did you have the feeling that you were part of that blog's community, or did you still feel like mainly just a reader of that blog? Did anyone respond to your comment?

What Does It Mean to Do Inquiry?

As students and teachers become familiar with the rudiments of blogging, some are ready to move to the deeper levels that may be served by these new media. Zac Chase, English teacher at the Science Leadership Academy (SLA) in Philadelphia, describes that his uses of Web 2.0 are in complete alignment with the school's core principles: inquiry, research, collaboration, presentation, and reflection, and that these core principles are more important than any Web 2.0 tool. "Each of our grade levels has three essential questions, and these are across the grade level," reports Zac. The teachers select texts that provide for good investigation of the essential questions and that are engaging. They do not abandon the literary canon. For example, in ninth grade when the essential question deals with identity, the students study *Hamlet* and *The Odyssey*. "The question we just finished up with is, 'What is the relationship between self and the world when all the world is seemingly changing?'"

To support this inquiry, the students read such books as *The Things They Carried* (O'Brien, 1990); *What Is the What* (Eggers, 2006); and *The Color of Water* (McBride, 1996); as well as the classics *The Crucible*, *The Taming of the Shrew*, and *The Great Gatsby*. "We don't feel beholden to the canon," says Zac.

The lessons within the technology course (required for each ninth grader) are made to match what is being taught in the content teachers' classrooms. "There's the adaptability in kids when you give them the tools of inquiry," says Zac who describes a typical class period as containing three to four activities, including some writing and an activity that gets them out of their seats. All the students have Drupal accounts. (Drupal is a platform for managing content and discussions, similar to Moodle and other Intranets.) "Not all teachers use them," says Zac. "I don't use them every day. They're there when I need them." The goal is not to use the latest technology; the goal is getting kids into the habit of doing inquiry as well as the other core activities of the school mentioned earlier.

SOCIAL ACTION PROJECT

Inquiry: What is an issue affecting you at the local, state, national, or global level that you can work to change?

Research:

- Identify the social, historical, and scientific factors surrounding this issue.
- Identify realistic steps that can be taken to create positive change regarding this issue.
- Identify a change agent with capital (social, political, or economic) necessary to work to improve the status of your issue.

Collaboration: While conducting your research, you will identify and subscribe to at least three Really Simple Syndication (RSS) feeds from viable sources regarding your topic. Throughout the quarter, you will synthesize your information in the form of at least 10 blog posts to your SLA Drupal blog. Two of these posts must analyze the topic through the scientific lens, and two of these posts must examine the topic through a sociological or historic lens. You will also be responsible for subscribing to and commenting on the blog postings of two members of your stream as well as two members of the opposite stream.

Presentation: Based on your research and synthesis, you will create a three- to- five-minute "elevator pitch" designed to convince your identified change agent to act on your issue. You will also create a research-based action plan outlining realistic steps that can be taken to improve conditions surrounding your issue.

Reflection: Given the cumulative nature of the understanding gained through this project, you will post five reflective posts charting your progress throughout the quarter with the fifth post to follow completion of the presentation portion.

Skill Sets

Necessary Tech Skills

Posting blog entries to Drupal

Searching and identifying reliable information sources

Subscribing to RSS feeds

Necessary Social Skills

Contacting change agent

Arranging face time with change agent

Providing productive feedback and support to peers

Pennsylvania State English Standards

1.1.11.A. Locate various texts, media, and traditional resources for assigned and independent projects before reading.

1.2.11.A. Read and understand essential content of informational texts and documents in all academic areas.

1. Differentiate fact from opinion across a variety of texts by using complete and accurate information, coherent arguments, and point of view.
2. Distinguish between essential and nonessential information across a variety of sources, identifying the use of proper references or authorities, and propaganda techniques where present.
3. Use teacher- and student-established criteria for making decisions and drawing conclusions.
4. Evaluate text organization and content to determine the author's purpose and effectiveness according to the author's theses, accuracy, thoroughness, logic, and reasoning.

1.4.11.B. Write complex informational pieces (e.g., research papers, analyses, evaluations, essays).

1. Include a variety of methods to develop the main idea.
2. Use precise language and specific detail.
3. Include cause and effect.
4. Use relevant graphics (e.g., maps, charts, graphs, tables, illustrations, photographs).
5. Use primary and secondary sources.

1.4.11.C. Write persuasive pieces.

1. Include a clearly stated position or opinion.
2. Include convincing, elaborated, and properly cited evidence.
3. Develop reader interest.
4. Anticipate and counter reader concerns and arguments. Include a variety of methods to advance the argument or position.

1.5.11.B. Write using well-developed content appropriate for the topic.

1. Gather, determine validity and reliability of, analyze, and organize information.
2. Employ the most effective format for purpose and audience.
3. Write fully developed paragraphs that have details and information specific to the topic and relevant to the focus.

1.4.11.D. Maintain a written record of activities, course work, experience, honors and interests.

Source: Zac Chase, Science Leadership Academy, Philadelphia.

RUBRIC FOR SOCIAL ACTION PROJECT

Name

Post

Post #

Stream

Post synthesizes viable outside sources to augment writer's knowledge (3 points)

Post includes properly cited direct quotation(s) (2 points)

Post includes properly cited indirect quotation(s) (2 points)

Post includes three or fewer conventional errors (spelling, grammar, punctuation, etc.) (3 points)

Post includes link(s) to material for supplemental reading (1 point)

Total:

Notice that the rubric for this activity does not include criteria related to the technology. For instance, there is no criterion such as "Correct use of RSS feed." In fact, all of the criteria could show up in an old-fashioned term paper. It's also worth noting that this assignment can be fully supported by the Pennsylvania State English standards, thus deflating the argument that some teachers make that there is "no room" in their day for these kinds of activities (because it's claimed the standards don't support them).

Many teachers at the SLA see blogs as places for storing student work and for documenting the processes of that work. This student work can form a research base not only for current students but also for students who are behind. Zac describes, "There's an assignment where they have to write multiple position papers and then take it on to the next level to post their paper on their blog and tag it so that it's searchable. Schools aren't necessarily using blogs as effectively as they should be by using the tag function so that those entries can be searchable."

tags

Most blogging hosts allow the blogger to create "tags" or informal categories for each entry. If a blogger writes an entry about a river cleanup in their local area, this entry could be tagged as "Cuyahoga River," "water ecology," and "pollution," to name a few possibilities. Some bloggers create a "Tag Cloud" on their blogs that automatically shows the prevalence of certain tags on their blogs, therefore showing the reader what topics are most commonly discussed.

Zac's colleague at the SLA, Kenneth Rochester, explains that he uses both Google Docs (a file sharing platform) and blogging to structure inquiry in his math classroom by dividing students into groups of four. "At the conclusion of the class, each group is responsible for posting their solutions to their classwork problems on their group's Google Doc," Ken says. "Before the start of the next class, I select one group's Google Doc to serve as the answer key for the class." Not only are that group's correct solutions displayed in class the next day, but also the problems that the group got wrong are assigned as homework. Each group member must contribute and show his or her work. Kenneth also keeps a class blog at blogspot.com that contains the daily notes, with students expected to tag their entries appropriately so that they can be searched. In addition, Kenneth is an active part of the math blogosphere himself, often checking in on selected blogs related to math.

MATH BLOGS FOR TEACHERS

Darren Kuroptawa's blog: http://adifference.blogspot.com

Dan Meyer's blog: http://blog.mrmeyer.com

Jason Dyer's Invisible Math: http://www.hotchalk.com/mydesk/index.php/hotchalk-blog-by-jason-dyer-invisible-math

Maria Anderson's Teaching College Math: http://teachingcollegemath.com

Source: Selected by Kenneth Rochester.

QUESTIONS TO CONSIDER

1. Students of all ages sometimes express discomfort with taking part in learning activities that have no clear-cut "answer" or "solution" at the end. Why do you think some people are uncomfortable with these kinds of inquiry projects? What can teachers do to structure the activity in such a way that all learners can be successful?
2. Think about an inquiry project you have taken part in without the use of computer technology. What do blogs and file sharing platforms such as Google Docs add to the learning experience? What do they take away?

How Do We Evaluate What We Read?

Helping kids to be discerning Internet readers is, of course, probably even more important in a Web 2.0 age in which misinformation gets shared doubly quickly via everyone's social networks. To address this issue, Cassie Neumann, a Mass Media teacher in Brunswick, Ohio, developed a lesson with a colleague based on the concept of "urban legends"—those stories that become folkloric and are referred to as *memes* as they take on a life of their own on the Internet.

memes

If you have ever received a chain e-mail with a picture of a cute kitty or an off-color video, then you may have been exposed to a "meme," which stands to signify as a kind of Internet rumor that sweeps the globe. These memes often become urban legends, such as the one in which Bill Gates is supposedly giving away $100 to the first 1,000 people who respond. Memes can also change the lives of those who come to fame through them as in the recent example of the middle-aged triumph of singer Susan Boyle who performed "I Dreamed a Dream" on the television series *Britain's Got Talent* and, within days, had her life transformed by the fact that the video clip of her appearance had been viewed by millions. It is a mystery how certain memes come to be and become so powerful.

"Next time I do this assignment, I'd like to focus even more on how these stories are spread. I focused more on the whys this time. And maybe find some way to test how far an urban legend will spread using different forms of mass media."
—Cassie Neumann

In Cassie's assignment, she used the wiki as a place to store examples of e-rumors and urban legends that had actually been e-mailed to her. She also included a few links to Web sites that debunk urban legends as starter sources. Students had time in class to work in the computer labs and find sources that either spread or debunked a chosen urban legend. Students answer some questions about their research process and come together in groups, sharing their research and writing their own urban legends in the format of an e-rumor (or chain e-mail).

URBAN LEGENDS AND E-RUMORS: HOW THE INTERNET IS USED TO SPREAD FALSE INFORMATION

Part One: Computer Research

Find a story. Pick one urban legend and search the Web for information on your story.

Research several sources. Two sources are required (one that tells the story and one that attempts to "debunk" or identify the source). Write down these Web sites!

You must show me your two Web sites on your computer screen to move on to Part Two.

Part Two: Individual Written Work

This part may be started in class today or completed for homework tonight.
Complete the following:

1. List your two Web sites and label which one is a source and which one spreads the story. *(2 points)*
2. Summarize your urban legend. *(5 points)*
3. Why is this story an urban legend? What urban legend traits are present in your story? *(5 points)*
4. What is the story's appeal as an urban legend? (Does it play on our fears? Is it creative? Why is it a story that people would want to pass along?) *(5 points)*

Part Three: Group Work

In class tomorrow

Share your urban legends and findings from yesterday.

Make a list of common and major traits found in your group's urban legend.

Create a new urban legend using your list of major urban legend traits. Format your urban legend so that it resembles an e-rumor that was sent to a mass public via e-mail or other Internet source.

Source: Cassie Neumann, Brunswick High School, Brunswick, Ohio.

QUESTIONS TO CONSIDER

1. Have you ever participated in spreading a meme on the Internet? If so, why? What is the attraction of participating in meme culture?
2. What are some ways to evaluate something you receive on the Internet to determine whether it has legitimate information or not?

How Do We Discuss Issues With People Face-to-Face and Across the World?

One of the central advantages of relatively unfettered access to the blogosphere is the ability to connect with people across the world, including experts on whatever topic is being studied. Teachers may structure an assignment so that students visit and comment on blogs of various experts or may invite the expert to comment on the class's blog. William Chamberlain has noticed that one of the first obstacles to overcome when making this assignment is the shyness factor: Students may be reluctant to comment on blogs other than those of their classmates or people they know. William finds blogs from schools from New Zealand and China and makes them available to his students, and he says, "I have tried to get some of my students interested in commenting on those blogs, but they seem reluctant. They are commenting more on their classmates' blogs, though. I am hopeful that they will become comfortable enough to start reaching out to the other students' blogs."

Another challenge (common to many bloggers) is getting other people to read and comment on your blog. William attempted a writing project to connect with young writers across the world who might be interested in reacting to the work of Chris Van Allsburg.

MYSTERIES OF HARRIS BURDICK PROJECT

Chris Van Allsburg's excellent children's book *The Mysteries of Harris Burdick* has been a source of writing inspiration for my students for years. I honestly have never had more success getting my students to write than using this book as a story starter.

So, my question to you is, "Will you join us?" I want you to write a story based on one of Van Allsburg's pictures from *The Mysteries of Harris Burdick*. There are two rules to this assignment:

1. You must use the line that goes with the picture somewhere in your story.
2. The story must have something to do with the picture.

If you don't have a copy, this link will take you to Google Book Search of the story.

Write your story on your blog, or use Google Docs or some other online publishing and send me the link so my class can read it and so I can link to it. If you can't publish it online, e-mail it to me at wmchamberlain@gmail.com, and I will post it here on the blog. You can even record audio or video of you reading your story!

There is no reward except for the joy of writing and sharing with others and perhaps the coveted *Blogging Tiger Award for Writing* to place on your blog or Web site.

Source: William Chamberlain, Noel Elementary School, Noel, Missouri.

William reports, however, that he never got any response from outsiders for this Chris Van Allsburg project. "While it is slightly disappointing, I understand that it may not fit in every teacher's curriculum, and kids don't always want to write if they don't have to. I am still hopeful that I may have one or two write a story."

George Mayo did a similar project that was more successful. It made use of Twitter even though he doesn't use Twitter at all in his middle school classroom. George set up an account on Twitter called "Manyvoices." Students in six different countries collaborated on writing a story, entry by entry, until they had 140 entries, each consisting of 140 (or fewer) characters (that is to say, key strokes, not fictional "characters"). The collaborative story was then published on Lulu.com. Another way of attracting viewers to a class site is to upload podcasts to that site. George has had students in his class record podcasts based on research they've done on life for kids in Vietnam. Through contacts he has in that country, George solicits comments from Vietnamese students on their podcasts, thus opening up a dialogue with young people from across the world.

There are many published reports of projects in which K–12 students have connected with authors online (see Richardson, 2003, for example) or university students (Borsheim, 2004). Teachers from the United States are also often impressed by the lead that teachers overseas—mainly in the United Kingdom, Australia, New Zealand, and Canada—have taken. Jody Hayes, fifth-grade teacher in a Catholic school in New Zealand, has been blogging with her students online for several years now. "All of our school computers are Internet accessible all of the time. . . . We have a 'trust' system where the children are allowed to blog and search with the class teacher there, and they report any inappropriate material right away. The more we have blogged, the more our school community has understood and enjoyed it. It has opened up the whole world for us." Jody believes that teaching Internet safety in authentic contexts is very important and all of her students, who have ranged in age from 5 to 11, are able to talk about things not to do online.

"No issues for us to date," she says. "Just motivated, engaged writers who await comments, appreciate feedback, know they are being read, are able to blog, Skype, share themselves, and be part of the conversation."

Second-year teacher Mike Slowinski from West De Pere High School in De Pere, Wisconsin, was inspired by some of these accounts of new media teachers and has used Google Groups to facilitate online literature circles. Mike reports, "It has been a big success for me so far because I've been able to take the idea of dialogue journals and use them to connect classrooms across great distances." Mike has invited preservice teachers from the University of Wisconsin–Eau Claire (UWEC) to join his class literature circles.

Mike describes this as a win-win situation, in that his students get to practice taking part in meaningful discussions with college students, and the college students who are future teachers get practice having conversations about books with teenagers using "a medium that resembles their own recreational communication tools."

When asked how he grades these online discussions, Mike responds that he talks with the students about the characteristics of deep literary discussions and does minilessons based around some of the comments that have been posted in the discussions. "I feel like that way," he says, "students get the chance to define effective discussions for themselves, and the groups have become very student-centered and directed rather than teacher directed." Mike also podcasts the introductions to the group and uploads them to the group site, and all culminating activities are assigned and uploaded through Google Groups.

ONLINE LITERATURE CIRCLES: EXPECTATIONS AND REQUIREMENTS

Posting

- Each week during the literature circles, you will be required to post:
    - Four comments and/or responses to other peoples' questions, including at least one response to the UWEC group leader
    - Two discussion questions of your own
- We will be posting for five weeks, so you will be expected, as a minimum, to post 20 responses and 10 questions of your own, as well as a possible podcast or two.
- You will also be assigned a final project by the UWEC group leader. The due date for this assignment is *Wednesday, November 12*. The assignment will be evaluated by the UWEC student, but the final decision on the grade will be up to me.

Grading

- Weekly requirements for posting will be due on each Saturday at 11:59 p.m.
- Each week you can receive a possibility of 30 points for posts.
- The final project is worth 50 points.
- Total Posting Points: 150 points
- Final Project Points: 50 points

Just because you post does not mean that you will earn all of the points. You will also be graded on the quality and quantity of your posts. Be sure to fully explain your thoughts, demonstrate your depth of understanding, and ask thought-provoking questions as you post.

You are encouraged to do posting outside of our Wednesday computer lab time. You can access Google Groups anywhere you can get on the Internet.

Extra Credit

- There will be two points of extra credit awarded for every additional post within the week's requirement.
- Extra posts must still be in-depth. They can either be thought-provoking questions, links to related articles or Web sites, or comments and/or responses to other peoples' questions or comments.

Online Etiquette

Maybe for the first time in your school careers, if you do not read your book, it affects more than just you. This online experiment will also impact the way that this course and others at West De Pere are taught in the future. It is a reflection of my teaching ability to my college professor and a reflection of West De Pere High School and the type of students that go here. It will also affect how these future teachers view teaching and high school students, as well as ongoing professional research and presentations, not only by me but also by Dr. Manning. This project is also a "test-drive" of allowing technological freedom at West De Pere High School. In order to participate in this, your computers were authorized to create a Google account, have an e-mail address, and access certain Google sites that were previously blocked. The results of this project could potentially affect the types of Web sites future West De Pere students will be able to access, as well as the possibility of opening up the conversation about students and school e-mail. Please keep all of this in mind as you interact online.

Any inappropriate behavior in Google Groups, over e-mail, or in any other fashion during this unit (as determined by me or the university professor) will result in immediate consequences. For sure, you will lose points, and depending on the situation, you may also lose your privilege to access Google Groups. If you are kicked out of Google Groups, you will fail this unit. You can certainly have fun on the discussion board, but keep in mind, this is still an academic experience. The main purpose is to discuss the book. However, if that is all we do on there, I feel as if we would not be using this site to its full potential. Feel free to interact with your group members, get to know them, ask appropriate questions about college, and so on. This should be a fun experience for everyone as long as we remember the main reason we're doing it.

Characteristics of Good Responses

- Builds off of others' ideas
- Connections to self—connections explained through textual evidence
- Connections to society—connections explained through textual evidence
- Quotes
- Supplemental readings
- Fully explains ideas

Things to Improve On

- Repetition
- Unanswerable questions
- Too many predictions
- Show me that you've read
- Back up claims with evidence and/or explanation from the text

Source: Mike Slowinski, West De Pere High School, De Pere, Wisconsin.

Mike has noticed that even though he didn't expect this, the students' responses fell into model kinds of discussion responses, such as "Connecting Self to Text" and "Making Connections to Other Texts." Mike collected some feedback from his students about these online discussions, and they were extremely positive. One of the main comments was that the 24/7 nature of the assignment allowed them to have time to think and craft their responses less quickly rather than to try to come up with a meaningful comment in the middle of a hectic classroom period. One student wrote, "You don't have to wait for a time to talk," and another said, "You don't have to feel embarrassed about anything you say."

Collaborative projects that seek to connect students across space and time often have social justice themes. Clarence Fisher is involved in a project that pairs his school with a school in Los Angeles in a collaborative called "Thinwalls," in which "students work together as a single class every day and see themselves as a single class even though they are separated by over three thousand miles." On some days, Clarence reports this contact is live, with teachers collaborating on lessons and delivering them live to each other's classes. "On other days, the contact may be asynchronous as students read and leave comments on each other's Weblogs or other multimedia productions." The students are working on projects meant to get at issues such as urban and rural living and life in America and life in Canada.

An ambitious project that attempted to increase cross-school collaboration was Tom Daccord's "Great Debate" project, which took place during the 2008 U.S. presidential election. As Tom describes it, "The Great Debate was designed to create a forum in which students from around the country could come together and share information and discuss and debate the issues." For the first part of this two-part project, Tom created blank pages on a wiki focusing on such pivotal campaign issues as economics and immigration. Students were then to provide background info on these issues, outline candidate positions, and include any type of resource (multimedia or otherwise) to help other students understand the issues. Each participating classroom was expected to contribute at least one page on this wiki but was also welcome to contribute to all pages. Tom reports, "The students were creating the content and teaching other students using the wiki. Students who were reviewing content on the Web page could edit it to correct errors or add supplemental information. It was very student centered." In the end, the project involved 25 teachers and 146 student members of the network, representing eight states.

GREAT DEBATE 2008 STUDENT HANDOUT

Student Participation in the Great Debate of 2008 Project

- The Great Debate of 2008 project is student centered, which means that most of the information and commentary is *supplied by students* and viewed by other students.

- The success of the project depends on *your* contributions and those of various other students, many of which you may never meet in person.
- As part of the Great Debate of 2008 project, you will contribute information pertaining to (at least) one campaign issue to our collaborative Great Debate of 2008 wiki.
- Depending on your teacher's objectives, you will examine all or some of the wiki pages developed by other students to learn more about campaign issues and candidate positions.
- You will also join The Great Debate of 2008 private online social network where you can meet other students involved in the project to discuss a range of campaign issues.
- At the private online social network you can start a discussion or participate in an existing one and participate in online polls and surveys.
- You can also watch videos about the candidates and add multimedia that pertains to the election.
- Your classroom will be judged on the quantity and quality of its contributions to both the wiki and the online social network, and you may win a prize as a result of those contributions.

Technical Information

- You will receive two separate e-mail invitations: one that will give you permission to edit our wiki pages and the other to participate in our private online social network.
- You will need to learn how to edit a wiki page, a relatively simple process. You may consult our video tutorial on how to edit a page at wikispaces.com.
- If you inadvertently delete information on a wiki page, it is possible to revert back to an earlier version of that same page. Please notify me via my contact form so that I can make any necessary corrections.
- To view YouTube videos at school, you may need to secure permission from a teacher or IT administrator.
- If you encounter a technical difficulty, please tell your teacher. You may also contact me via my contact form.

Code of Conduct

- By participating in the Great Debate of 2008 project, you agree to use our wiki and online social network for academic purposes only related to the 2008 presidential election.
- You agree not to use profane, sexually explicit, racist, sexist, or hurtful language or materials.
- You agree to refrain from using personally identifiable information—such as your last name, home address, personal e-mail address, home telephone number, and the like—when signing up for the 2008 wiki and private online social network.

(Continued)

(Continued)

- You agree not to invite or include others in the project who have not been explicitly invited to participate.
- Please note that the project is continually monitored, and any inappropriate language or materials will be removed, and the responsible student(s) may be punished.
- You agree to abide by these rules; your signature at the bottom of this page signals your acceptance of the regulations that govern your participation in the Great Debate of 2008 project. (Your teacher will collect signatures.)

Your signature: ______________________________

Source: Tom Daccord, Boston, Massachusetts.

Once students had contributed a wiki page, they were free to read other wiki pages, and then they were to go into the online social network that Tom set up as a Ning (on Ning.com) in which students could start discussions or post videos. Tom started 20 topics for discussion himself but was pleased that students added around 15 more topics.

"I was encouraged that students were taking the initiative while others were joining in the conversation," Tom says. "One of the most popular topics was the death penalty. There were many replies. One of the beauties of the assignment was that they moved in areas I didn't anticipate, like the death penalty." In addition, students not only posted videos they had found but also videos they had made.

When asked about what kind of a rubric could be designed for a project like this, Tom answered, "Ideally the kids will create something that exceeds our expectations." However, he did suggest some general criteria: looking at students' contributions to the wiki and the Ning, the level of research and critical thinking skills demonstrated, and whether the students were able to discuss and write about that information they contributed to the wiki in a lucid, clear, and persuasive manner. Tom warned against grading individual blog entries on the Ning, as students might feel it was the opinions they expressed in the blogs that were being assessed.

One challenge of the project was students' confusing the purpose of the wiki and the Ning. The Ning was the space in the project that was more appropriate for expressing opinions rather than the wiki, which was meant to be as objective as possible. Tom reports that he advised teachers to move some highly personal expressions of opinion posted by students on the wiki to the Ning, instead.

One of the teachers who took part in the project, Scott Warren, a social studies teacher from Girls Preparatory School in Chattanooga, Tennessee, says, "I think there's great potential to take the energies the kids have for these platforms and channel them. The faces of my students displayed the excitement and fire that every teacher looks for when initiating an engaging project." Scott reports that his students especially enjoyed the social networking aspect of the project and that some students are still keeping in touch with some of the contacts they made.

Paul Allison's YouthVoices project (http://youthvoices.net/home) is another project that is attempting to foster long-distance collaborations beyond the span of just one project. Paul is an English teacher in Flushing, New York; coming out of the work he did in the New York Writing Project, he created a space for students to discuss and collaborate over the span of several years. Paul also produces a Webcast each Wednesday available at TeachersTeachingTeachers (http://teachersteachingteachers.org)—a weekly Webcast that brings together teachers from across the world who are interested in social media. A recent episode brought together two Spanish language teachers from Colorado and Connecticut, a 10th-grade student from New York, an English-as-a-foreign-language teacher from Mexico, and an English teacher from New Jersey. These conversations are recorded and made available as podcasts on the Web site.

Currently, Paul teaches sophomore and junior English. Paul starts the year by having the kids read a lot of magazine and online articles. Students blog about their reading individually and in literature circles, also known as "inquiry groups," that he hosts on the Youth Voices Web site. Teaching in New York, Paul still has to prepare the students for the famous statewide Regents exam; he says the test is not difficult for most of his students, but one third of his students are ESL students who have been in the United States for less than two years, and for them, the test is challenging. This is also why, he says, he has had to structure some of his online writing activities in a more deliberate manner.

While YouthVoices is public (able to be viewed by anyone who has the Web address), only students' first names are listed. There is also the option of having completely private discussion groups within the site, if so desired by the teacher. On the site, there are "inquiry groups" that focus on topics as diverse as anime, emo music, and "catastrophe and resilience" ("a place where we can take a stand against historical and current atrocities, genocides, ethnic cleansings, holocausts, occupations, and wars"). When you click on one of the "inquiry groups," you are directed to a page that has one of the following four categories: current assignments, group discussions, images, and bookmarks. Students are free to add to any and all of the four categories.

"We're not even calling this a blog anymore," says Paul, "[the kids] post onto a site. What their blog ends up being is anything they post in reverse order." Another feature of participation is that students may, whenever they post something, send the post through to Twitter and all of the followers of YouthVoices receiving the posting. Students are provided models for several different kinds of responses from "General Discussion" to "How to Comment on Audio" to "Doing Digital Annotations on Diigo."

Paul feels that this kind of very structured response helps to scaffold for kids who really need that extra support when writing online.

GENERAL DISCUSSION RESPONSE

Dear <first name of poster>:
I <*past tense verb* showing emotion> your <post/poem/essay/letter/image . . . >, "<exact title>," because . . . <add two or three sentences>.

One sentence you wrote that stands out for me is "<quote from message.>" I think this is <adjective> because . . . <add one or two sentences>.

Another sentence that I <past tense verb> was "<quote from message>." This stood out for me because . . . .

Your <post/poem/essay/letter/image . . . > reminds me of something that happened to me. One time . . . <add three or four sentences telling your own story>.

Thanks for your writing. I look forward to seeing what you write next, because . . . <add two or three sentences explaining what will bring you back to see more about this person's thoughts>.

Agree or Disagree Response

Dear <first name of poster>:
I <*past tense verb* showing emotion> your <poem/post/image/letter . . . >, "<exact title>," because . . . <add two or three sentences>.

One sentence you wrote that stands out for me is "<quote from message>." I think this is <adjective> because . . . <add one or two sentences>.

Another sentence that I <past tense verb> was "<copy a sentence or line from the post>." This stood out for me because . . . .

I do/don't <adverb> agree with you that . . . . One reason I say this is . . . . Another reason I agree/disagree with you is . . . .

Thanks for your writing. I look forward to seeing what you write next, because . . . <add two or three sentences explaining what will bring you back to see more about this person's thoughts>.

Letters to the President Activity

1. Go here: http://www.letters2president.org.
2. Find a letter that you would like to respond to and read it.
3. Copy the URL of that letter.
4. Copy the "Agree or Disagree Response Guide" into a new discussion and write to that student.

5. Ater you type that stdent's title from this Web site, make it into a link by
   - highlighting the title,
   - clicking on the link icon (looks like a globe with a chain link), and
   - pasting the URL that you copied in Step 2.
6. Finish the sentence starters with your own thoughts and post this on YouthVoices.

Source: From YouthVoices.

Even though suggestions for the responses are somewhat structured for the kids and so could be easily assessed, Paul isn't too concerned with grading. For this project, he says that he doesn't feel that his assessment is all that important. "Part of what is amazing," he states, "is when they're in a social network, they really do want to do what another student did. There's a kind of pressure that's peer driven. Assessment is about self-assessment in the end."

Some other educators I talked to saw the opportunities for assessment in the use of social networking platforms. Elizabeth Helfant, a former chemistry teacher who now has the title of Instructional Technologist at the Upper School of the Mary Institute and Saint Louis Country Day School, shepherds a variety of Web 2.0 projects in her school. These cross-curricular areas range from an interdisciplinary course focusing on the Sudan that allows students to use raw footage from National Geographic to make documentaries about the crisis, to a Scribe in Math project in which students rotate taking notes on the day's lesson as they build a companion Web site for the entire math course.

Elizabeth's teachers noticed that the interface between a user and a Ning is very similar to that between a user and Facebook. Some of the teachers took inspiration from this similarity and built a project focusing on the Jacksonian period in U.S. History. "Kids all get logins like 'Bronson Alcott' with the password 'Brookfarm,'" says Elizabeth. "They then play 'Facebook' as their character for a week with some research tasks mixed in."

JACKSONIAN REFORMERS FACEBOOK

You are to create a Facebook page for one of the reformers listed on the next page. As you are assuming the identity of the person, all entries should be in first person. You will have both class and homework time to work on your Facebook page on Wednesday, Thursday, and Friday, November 12 to 14. The assignment is due on Monday, November 17, 2008.

(Continued)

(Continued)

Project Requirements:

1. *Profile*: Create a profile for your reformer, including a picture.
2. *Annotated Bibliography*: Turn in an annotated bibliography of at least three sources correctly cited in MLA format. Your sources should come from the databases and the print resources in McCulloch Library. Pictures, music, and video (if used) should be cited in MLA format in a separate media index.
3. *Blog*: You should write a blog entry from your reformer's point of view on each of the questions listed below. (You may write one entry on each topic or combine several of the topics for a more detailed entry. However, you must have more than one blog entry.)
    - What *criticisms* of American society did the individual have?
    - What *methods* did the person use to improve American life?
    - What *successes* and/or *failures* did the individual have in promoting reform?
    - What were the major *beliefs* of the individual?
    - How *influential* was the reformer during his or her lifetime?
    - What *influences* in your early life led you to be a reformer?
4. *Visuals and Music*: You must include a picture of your reformer in the profile and must post at least one other picture and/or video illustrating your character's area of reform. You are also encouraged to post music relating to your reformer's theme or the time period, if relevant. Be sure to include captions that link your pictures, videos, and music to the reformer.
5. *Comments*: In the character of your reformer, you must reply to four other Facebook pages, one from each category. Your response should include
    - areas of agreement between you and the other reformer,
    - areas of disagreement between you and the other reformer, and
    - an evaluation of the other reformer's contribution to bettering the United States.

Your page should include information up to 1850—many of these reformers were active after 1850 and during the Civil War, but you should focus on their pre-1850 work. Lastly, remember that Facebook pages are designed to be interesting and entertaining as they let you get to know a person!

Signing into Ning: Your Facebook Web page is located at http://facebookfederman.ning.com. E-mail login is firstinitial_lastname@ai.micds.org, and password is reformer+initials. So for example, Samuel Gridley Howe would be s_howe@ai.micds.org and reformersgh.

Jacksonian Reformers Facebook Project Sign-Up

Education

Samuel Gridley Howe—

Horace Mann—

Thomas Gallaudet—

Women

Lucretia Mott—

Dorothea Dix—

Elizabeth Cady Stanton—

Abby Kelley—

Abolition

Frederick Douglass—

Elijah Lovejoy—

William Lloyd Garrison—

Utopians

John Humphrey Noyes—

Joseph Smith—

Bronson Alcott—

Source: Lesley McIntire, Carla Beard Federman, and Elizabeth Helfant, Mary Institute and Saint Louis Country Day School.

Elizabeth, a former chemistry teacher, also describes how the science teachers in her school use wikis to assess lab reports: "The wiki allows the teacher to see exactly who did what part and when it was done, and the wiki also offers students a discussion area to negotiate the lab results. Teachers can watch as the lab report is created and can also offer students feedback during the process using the discussion tab." Helfant views the wiki as serving to aid the teacher to monitor work levels of various group members. "Keeping track of student progress may also be aided by using Google Notebook with the 'Clip to Notebook' add-on," says Helfant, allowing the teacher and librarian to monitor the research that the student is doing. "Everything that they collect electronically, text and images, can be highlighted, and when the students right click, they get an option to send it to their notebook." There is also a space for the teacher to make comments and potentially guide further research. "It provides a means for assessing the skill that is being taught while it is being taught," she says.

QUESTIONS TO CONSIDER

1. How do school-based social networks differ from out-of-school social networks? What does each have to offer?
2. Do you communicate and collaborate differently with someone in an in-school social networking project versus an out-of-school social networking project? How so?
3. What are some ways you have learned to negotiate the Web so that you are able to connect with experts and potential colleagues from all over the world? Is such collaboration worth it to your learning and well-being, or is setting it up more trouble than it's worth?

In this chapter, projects have been described that can be created in schools that don't have an excessive amount of filtering. Interestingly, it's apparent that there are certainly safeguards for kids in place, and one could argue, almost a surveillance function coming out of some of these projects, even in these educational settings that are relatively free of barriers and filters of online communication. Educators in these kinds of situations are, of course, still struggling to use these new media in settings and in the context of old paradigms, and this may serve to set up interesting contrasts and a tension that may be worth teasing apart. There will be more about this potential conflict in Chapter 6. But first, in Chapter 5, projects will be described that test the limits of a filter-less approach to Web 2.0 classroom applications, with all the logistical, legal, and ethical dilemmas that those increasing freedoms bring.

A Blog Post From the Field

We could have picked up litter, we could have had a bake sale, and we could have raked leaves. We chose to help stop world hunger. Each year our students at Edgewood High School in Edgewood, Maryland, are required to complete a service learning project where students have to serve the community while enriching their minds. In the past, projects have been done that made an impact in the local community, but we wanted to do something that would show our students that one person can impact the world.

This year, the English department came up with the idea to earn rice from the World Food Programme's Web site to help aid starving people and nations. In addition to earning rice, our students wrote reflections and researched information about this problem. By thinking about what it means to be truly hungry and consider who it is that is being helped, our students were inspired and motivated to help the world. We used a "wiki," a free educational Web site creator, for students to reflect (view ours at http://ehsfreerice .pbwiki.com). While the intention of the site was to be environmentally conscious and keep students from misplacing their work, it connected our school in a way we were not expecting. All students have their own Web pages on the site where they make it their own. In a world where teenagers are extremely techno-savvy, they embraced the site and even preferred it to a booklet of questions. Freshman Kevin Price agrees that "service learning is the most fun and educational service learning project that I've done yet."

Our school goal was to earn 1.3 million grains of rice by the end of May. We began this project the first week of February, and we have already met our goal within the first month. Our students have gone further than what is asked of them and are earning thousands of grains of rice on their own time. With mice clicking furiously to answer rice questions, students are not just learning vocabulary words, they are learning what impression one person can make on the world. Koraun Chase, junior, says, "Free rice has taught me that even the littlest of things can help a family or person on the other side of the world."

As of today, our school is almost at 3 million grains of rice, over double our yearly goal, and we still have two whole months left. Brian Calderon-Ordonez, freshman, thinks,

"By doing this, we see how other people are being helped and lives are being changed. It's not about getting a high score; it's about changing the world." We asked our students to do their part, and they heeded the call, one grain of rice at a time.

Kim Whitaker
English Teacher
Edgewood High School
Edgewood, Maryland

5

"*Venti*"

Social Networking in an Unlimited Tech Environment

Some teachers are able to work in a kind of filter-less bliss. For these teachers, they don't need to worry about having to mimic Web 2.0. They can use the real thing live, seemingly with few difficulties. Also, this chapter includes some "off-campus" settings in which Web 2.0 activities may be housed—such settings as libraries, afterschool clubs, film festivals, and home schools. And this chapter includes a profile of an adventurous school that has gone to a hybrid schedule in which some students spend class time at home.

How Do We Use Facebook to Learn What We Need to Learn?

After months of looking, there was only one teacher I could find who admitted to using Facebook unfiltered within the school day in a K–12 setting, and even this teacher said that it "flew under the radar screen" of his school's administrators. I found several teachers who said that their students had created Facebook groups centered around a class or a project, almost as a study group, but I found only one teacher who used Facebook as part of a school assignment. This teacher is Brett Moller, and he is Head of Learning and Educational Technologies at Kings Christian College in Gold Coast, Queensland, Australia. (In Australia, the term *college* is often used for a K–12 school, usually private. Brett's school is private and serves children from ages 5–18.)

Brett was working as a media teacher at his previous school when he used Facebook in a project with another teacher who taught religion. The religion teacher expressed a desire to use media more in his classroom, and Brett showed him Facebook. For several years, Brett had been having his students post their final films on Facebook. Brett had connected with a group of media professionals who gave his students positive feedback about their films (all done through Facebook). As Brett explains it, "I showed this teacher, and he got excited. The idea was to get students who were doing a unit on theoretical ethics and ethical issues to learn a small amount of the content well enough to teach it to the rest of the class in a creative and effective way." Each student was given a prompt related to an ethical issue, such as slavery in the cocoa industry, for example. Students were expected to research both sides of the ethical situation and then communicate their own ideas in blogs and podcasts. "Facebook was used to connect the group members with the experts in the given fields, most of whom were professors in areas of ethics or philosophy," Brett describes.

As each group began to blog and produce podcasts about their issue, some local university professors played a crucial role. The professors, who were "keen about the project," says Brett, began to generate some critical thinking on the site by posting some "devil's advocate" arguments, trying to suggest, for example, that stopping slavery would mean the end of candy bars, as we know them. The religion teacher also created an anonymous profile that became his alter ego. "He used this pretend profile to generate extremist views and give opposing views," explains Brett.

At the end of the unit, the teacher revealed that he had created this alter ego and then gave an old-fashioned test over the material. Brett and his colleague noticed significant improvement in student performance, particularly among students who normally did C work. "We had a debrief afterward and had a chat room," reports Brett. They said, "The reason it worked is that we were able to discuss this with our friends. Having media as a part of it was a great benefit and being able to get them."

When I asked about security issues, Brett responded that the Facebook group was set up in a completely secure way, with only the students (and the university professors) being allowed to comment. Brett claims that he only had one parent complaint about the project, and when he showed her that it's impossible for an outsider to log into the group, she was satisfied with the project's safety. He did admit there were some challenges to this project. "You still have to be a vigilant teacher," he said. "At the beginning, kids were more interested in checking their own Facebook profiles."

Also, Brett pointed out that this project was kind of a mind-shift for the students, in that they had been trained that school is about "regurgitating information." One of the things that was brought up is that we need to do this with our younger students and try this project with them," Brett says, "so that students get used to more interactive, student-centered learning at an earlier age."

In his new job at Kings Christian College, Brett reports that some of the students have set up closed Facebook groups for his class in which students start discussions about the assignments and other parts of the class. Brett takes part occasionally in this Facebook study group, feeling that it efficiently cuts down on the number of e-mails he has to send to students—he can just post an announcement on the group's page. Brett reports that the students who set this up also put all the due dates for the class into the Facebook calendar, meaning that any time they log onto their Facebook account, they are reminded of upcoming due dates. "What I love about this is that we are bringing the learning to their world," Brett says, "not creating a second place that we inflict on them. Because they own this, they love it."

Brett feels that educators should be involved with social networking platforms such as Facebook almost as a pilot instructor would need to be in the cockpit with the student pilot. "You can write naughty notes with a paper and pencil, too," Brett says. "Now we just have another medium [to do so]. One of the issues I have spent some time investigating is the need to create a digital culture in your school and parent community."

This is the kind of analogy that's frequently used that compares the way we teach kids to be safe online to how we teach swimming or diving: that is, it makes no sense to teach kids to be safe online by preventing them from being online. This would be like trying to teach someone to swim on dry land or trying to teach someone to drive by sitting them down on a sofa and getting them to hold a mock wheel.

QUESTIONS TO CONSIDER

1. Is Facebook primarily to be used for fun—networking with friends, finding a boyfriend or girlfriend—or can it be used for educational purposes?
2. Is it appropriate for students and teachers to "friend" each other on Facebook or follow each other on Twitter? If not, why not?
3. Does the social networking experience become ruined when it is used, say, as a homework reminder system or for some other school-based task?

WHAT IS IT LIKE TO TELECOMMUTE?

Most of the assignments described in this book so far have some element to them that can be done outside the school day—whether responding to a blog entry or building a wiki text, students have the ability to work on these kinds of projects any time of the day or night. But why, in fact, do students have to come to school at all in a Web 2.0 world? What happens when a school allows students to do some work at home?

Elizabeth Boeser, of Jefferson High School in Minneapolis, assigns much of the same kind of work in her English class that has been described earlier in this book, especially in terms of her uses of blogs and wikis. What makes her situation different is that her school is piloting what are called "hybrid" courses, in which students are permitted to work on coursework off campus at their homes. The hybrid course has some face-to-face class meetings but not every day. Students are expected to do some of their work at home and, in fact, don't have to report to class every day. "Each hybrid teacher gets to determine when his or her classes meet," says Liz.

Sample One-Week Schedule

Monday	*Tuesday*	*Wednesday*	*Thursday*	*Friday*
Online or Small Group	Entire Class Together Live	Online or Small Group	Entire Class Together Live	Online or Small Group

Sample Three-Week Schedule

Monday	*Tuesday*	*Wednesday*	*Thursday*	*Friday*
9/1/08 NO SCHOOL	9/2/08 LARGE GROUP *Little Brother* Chapter 1 Rules/Schedule Parent Letter	9/3/08 LARGE GROUP *Little Brother* Chapter 2 Gmail Account/ E-mail Due *Growing Up Online*	9/4/08 LARGE GROUP *Little Brother* Chapter 3 Prompt for Application Essay Due	9/5/08 LARGE GROUP *Little Brother* Chapter 4 Invitation to Blogs Due Parent Signatures Due
9/8/08 SMALL GROUP MON *Little Brother* Chapter 5	9/9/08 LARGE GROUP *Little Brother* Chapter 6 Rough Draft Application Essay Due in class	9/10/08 SMALL GROUP WED *Little Brother* Chapter 7	9/11/08 LARGE GROUP *Little Brother* Chapter 8	9/12/08 SMALL GROUP FRI *Little Brother* Chapter 9
9/15/08 SMALL GROUP MON *Little Brother* Chapter 10	9/16/08 LARGE GROUP *Little Brother* Chapter 11	9/17/08 SMALL GROUP WED *Little Brother* Chapter 12 Application Essay Due online @ www.turnitin.com Begin Online Role-play	9/18/08 LARGE GROUP *Little Brother* Chapter 13 Application Final Essay Due in class w/ originality report Online Role-play	9/19/08 SMALL GROUP FRI *Little Brother* Chapter 14 Online Role-play

I wanted to find out more about this unique organizational structure, so I talked to John Weisser, Technology Coordinator for Jefferson High. John admitted that when they first started researching the idea, they couldn't find any high school that allowed for such a hybrid course, although many local universities and community colleges regularly offer these kinds of courses. "Many people I talked to had experiences taking (and sometimes teaching) online classes, and their opinions were almost uniformly negative."

But the school decided to pilot two hybrid courses the first year even with this kind of negative feedback and during the 2008–2009 school year were in the first full year of implementation, with about eight courses working in some sort of hybrid format. As of this writing, the school has not had any major problems with students taking advantage of this kind of schedule. Parents and students taking the hybrid courses must sign a permission letter that even asks them to rate themselves on time management and organization (see Appendix), and the school has communicated extensively with the community to explain the way the courses are taught.

Liz admits that many of her fellow teachers are afraid of this format and feel that the school should monitor when students are logging onto their computers at home, for example. "But these kids don't do their work at a certain time," Liz responds. "I don't care *when* they do their work."

So what does Liz assign in such a hybrid class, in which kids are not present every day? She starts by assigning blogs, both personal blogs and vlogs (blogs with a video component). She then brings in wikis and has students make a study guide for whatever book the class is reading. And Liz reports that she still assigns a lot of traditional writing assignments. Students also collaborate in groups of three on a research paper, and these are posted to their wikis. "The experience gives the students the efficacy to create their own study guides," says Liz. "I don't ever talk in class. I don't lecture ever. I just sit next to kids. The class turns into a workshop."

Liz also believes strongly in the use of role playing in her class, and using blogs and wikis allowed for a multimodal platform for that kind of role playing and one that could be up and running 24 hours a day, seven days a week, available for students to interact with the curriculum whenever they want.

WIKI ROLE PLAY ASSIGNMENT

Using Laurie Halse Anderson's *Speak* and Stephen Chbosky's *The Perks of Being a Wallflower*, in conjunction with our own real-world experiences, students will create characters based in a high school that we make up online. These characters will

(Continued)

(Continued)

interact in a role-play, which will happen in the space provided in our Schooled the Write Way blog. Remember that the character has to be someone involved in a high school in Honolulu, Hawaii, which is the city that was picked for the overall best information, links, and picture provided. This is our high school.

Directions:

Please use the information below and the data provided from Wikipedia—look at Charlie's Example in the sidebar to get an idea of what you should do for this assignment. The more information you have for your character, the better you will do on this. Copy the list below and make your own page. Name your page your character's name and create a link for it in the sidebar. You should also make some lists of your character's favorite things as is done on the Wikipedia page, and you should add pictures and links as one might do in Blogger, MySpace, or Facebook.

Character Name: ______________________________

Physical Description

Birth Date and Age: ______________________________

Height: ______________________________

Eye Color: ______________________________

Build: ______________________________

Weight: ______________________________

Hair Color: ______________________________

Sex/Gender: ______________________________

Physical Adjectives: ______________________________

Personality Type

Main Personality Traits: ______________________________

____

Disposition: ______________________________

____

Self-Image: ______________________________

____

Family

Marital Status: ______________________________

____

Children: ______________________________

____

Place in Family: ______________________________

____

Immediate Family Members: ______________________________

____

Relatives: ______________________________

____

Personal Data

Education: ______________________________

____

Occupation: ______________________________

____

Social Class: ______________________________

____

Religion: ______________________________

____

Ethnicity: ______________________________

____

Hobbies: ______________________________

____

Ambitions: ______________________________

____

Friends: ______________________________

____

(Continued)

(Continued)

Other

Favorite Color: ___________________________

Favorite Food: ___________________________

Favorite Beverage: ___________________________

Favorite Book: ___________________________

Favorite Time of Day: ___________________________

Favorite Day of the Week: ___________________________

Favorite Season: ___________________________

Car: ___________________________

Favorite Sport: ___________________________

Favorite Place to Go: ___________________________

Favorite Animal: ___________________________

Favorite Activity: ___________________________

After Liz had been using blogs and wikis for a few semesters, Rick Beach, her professor at University of Minnesota, suggested that she try using Ning.com as a site for online discussion. "The Ning allows for a totally different kind of discussion," Liz said. "Plus, kids were able to make alliances." As the topic for her first Ning, Liz decided to make the focus on school Internet usage policies, including both the access that students should be allowed to have and the access that staff should be allowed to have.

Students began to research and post to the Ning that certain Web sites were blocked at their school, including YouTube. They began to accumulate information about school censorship and policies about filtering in educational settings. Liz reports that the students ended up contacting administrators in their district. The dean of students came to class, and the students made policy recommendations. At last report, the students were also planning to make their arguments (for less-strict filtering) at their school's board meeting.

Students were evaluated both by Liz and by themselves on the quality of the posts they created on the Ning. The criteria for evaluating these posts sound like the criteria for any persuasive writing assignment: being able to clearly state an opinion and to support that opinion with convincing evidence (Table 5.1).

Table 5.1 Self-Evaluation of Posts to Ning

	4	*3*	*2*	*1*
1. Creation of a role Purposeful use of creative language (character voice, descriptive language)	Creates and portrays a highly believable, realistic, and relevant role through effective use of detailed descriptive language, images, and links	Creates and portrays a somewhat believable, realistic, and relevant role through use of descriptive language, images, and links	Creates a role with only limited believability, reality, and relevancy through limited use of descriptive language, images, and links	Creates and portrays a role that is not believable, realistic, or relevant with little or no use of descriptive language, images, and links
2. Statement of position	Makes a clear, forceful statement of position reflecting strong understanding of topic	Makes some statement of position reflecting some understanding of topic	Makes an unclear statement of position reflecting limited understanding of topic	Makes only a vague statement of position
3. Support for position Purposeful use of links and images within the context of the argument to develop role and/or argument	Provides extensive, elaborated evidence or reasons for position based on clearly defined description of the context	Provides some evidence or reasons for position based on a description of the context	Provides limited evidence or reasons for position with little description of the context	Provides no supporting evidence or reasons

(Continued)

Table 5.1 (Continued)

	4	*3*	*2*	*1*
4. Recognition of counter-arguments—statement of counter-position (particularly in comments)	Clearly identifies stated or potential counter-arguments in own words or clearly restates other role's positions in own words and formulates a strong refutation with extensive supporting evidence and/or reasons	Identifies stated or potential counter-arguments or restates other role's positions and formulates a refutation in own words with some supporting evidence and/or reasons	Identifies stated or potential counter-arguments or other role's positions by simply quoting or restating with a weak refutation	Identifies stated or potential counter-arguments or other role's positions by simply quoting or restating with no refutation
5. Seeks audience identification—use of audience appeals and builds alliances with other roles	Seeks audience identification through specific references to the audience/pronoun use, references to relationships with/stances that would appeal to audiences, or use of persona that would appeal to audiences in terms of benefits or advantages	Seeks audience identification through limited references to the audience/pronoun use, references to relationships with/stances that would have some appeal to audiences, or use of persona that would appeal to audiences	Seeks limited audience identification, but uses primarily "I" examples that do not reference the audiences' perspectives or potential benefits	Makes no attempt to seek audience identification.

Students were also expected to write a literary analysis paper and an MLA-formatted research paper, and the Ning became a place to house these projects. One paper the students were assigned required them to explain the problems and issues discussed in the Ning role-play (Figure 5.1). Students were expected to acknowledge and refute opposing arguments expressed during the activity.

Figure 5.1 Role Reflection

Role Name: ______________________ **Real Name:** ____________________ **Period:** _____

Role Reflection—First: Save this document to your desktop as your Last, First Name + Reflection (e.g., BoeserLizReflection). Second: Make sure you completely read and comprehend the questions before you answer them. Third: Please use a different font or color for your response. Fourth: You must complete the document in Neo Office or Pages, save your work again as a .DOC, which you can do if your export the document. Fifth: E-mail this document *as an attachment* to Ms. Boeser. Last: You must also copy and paste this entire reflection into Blogger.com. Name your posting as follows: Role-play Reflection.

1. Summarize your role's beliefs or stance on the issue(s). Do not simply regurgitate and/or copy and paste your answer from your bio.
2. Explain your use of language (the word choices and verbal style) you used to convey these beliefs or stances.
3. What strategies did you use while trying to convince the other characters (formulating counter arguments, building alliances)?
4. What evidence or reasons did you use to support your positions? In what ways were your evidence and reasons effective in convincing others to adopt your positions? How do you know?
5. When you received a reply that challenged or disagreed with your position, how did you typically respond to these challenges or disagreements?
6. Do you think that your arguments had any influence on your audiences' beliefs on this issue? If so, in what ways?
7. Based on your decisions regarding power in your Bubbl.us map, (see http://bubbl.us) explain the criteria you used to decide who had power. How did people use their power or gain more power?
8. You completed your self-assessment on your own work in the role-play. How does the criteria on the rubric help you understand what makes an effective argument?
9. You are writing a paper from your own personal perspective on issues with the current school policies on Internet use and access where you suggest possible solutions that will eventually be used to create some joint proposals to the school. How did this role-play prepare you to write this paper? In what ways did the knowledge that you would actually be writing to change school policies influence your involvement in this role-play?
10. Describe your overall positive and negative feelings about engaging in this role-play and give reasons for those feelings.

(Continued)

(Continued)

Rate your feelings about this role-play.

Not engaged.	1	2	3	4	5	6	Highly engaged.
Not comfortable in my role.	1	2	3	4	5	6	Very comfortable in my role.
Not familiar with the issue.	1	2	3	4	5	6	Very familiar with the issue.
Not personally concerned with the issue.	1	2	3	4	5	6	Highly concerned about this issue.
My role had little power.	1	2	3	4	5	6	My role had a lot of power.
My role was isolated.	1	2	3	4	5	6	My role felt connected.
The role-play didn't help me learn to argue.	1	2	3	4	5	6	The role-play really helped me learn to argue better.
I have had little previous experience in debate.	1	2	3	4	5	6	I have had a lot of debate experience.
The role-play didn't help prepare me for the paper.	1	2	3	4	5	6	The role-play really helped prepare me for the paper.
Knowing that I would be advising the school had no influence on my engagement.	1	2	3	4	5	6	Knowing that I would be advising the school had a strong influence on my engagement.

Liz repeatedly stressed her preference for using Nings rather than blogs to generate student discussion. "Ning has a blog and a forum. Each member of the Ning has his or her own page and can make them look a certain way." Liz feels that these kinds of assignments go deeper than the traditional product-driven high school activities. She feels that the students are already producing much at the high school level: "They're always turning in these huge projects," she says, "but the study and work that goes in to them is hurried and at a surface level. The students don't know how to research," she says. "It's no wonder they have difficulty with these new kinds of assignments. They don't have to get deep very often."

QUESTIONS TO CONSIDER

1. Think about your work habits. Do you tend to do your best work early in the morning, during the day, or late at night? What about your physical surroundings? Describe your ideal work setting and time of day.

2. Why have schools insisted on having physical custody of young people sometimes even as late as age 21? Are there legitimate reasons for this level of monitoring?

What Does Learning Look Like Outside of the School Day?

In my research for this book, I would often encounter educators who would tell me that they were using social networking tools but not within the school day. They found these tools to be enormously powerful and useful for teaching a kind of hidden curriculum, a curriculum that was seen as perhaps more appropriate for "afterschool" activities. Often these extracurricular uses of social media revolve around activities or groups that are seen as marginalized by the traditional school curriculum. Video games, for example, while being probably more suited to school than the general public might think (Gee, 2003), have not been seen as related to teaching and learning and have perhaps not been appreciated for their social networking applications. It has been educators who work with students in nonclassroom settings such as libraries or afterschool programs who seem to have much more freedom in using games and online social networking tools.

Some school media specialists have taken to sponsoring (old-fashioned) face-to-face clubs centered on gaming and game culture. Liz Martin, Media Specialist at Saluda Trail Middle School in Rock Hill, South Carolina, became interested in forming a gaming club when she began to play Massively Multiplayer Online Role-Playing Games (MMORPGs) herself. "I was fascinated how in the online games players will complete boring mundane tasks without complaint and be excited about it," she says. "As an educator, I ponder how we can capture that enthusiasm and transfer it to school. A gaming club seemed a natural step in that process."

She and her assistant Amanda Cavin began by previewing free games and then compiling a list that seemed to have educational value. They also bought a Wii game device that the kids were very excited about. The club meets every Monday morning before school in a computer lab and has been a huge hit. Liz thinks a large part of its popularity is simply the social aspect of the activity, noting that the club meetings are full of conversation before, during, and after the gaming experience. "I think those who view the games as a solitary endeavor are out of touch with gaming in the digital era," she says. "In my experience and observation, it is a very social activity. The whole basis of MMORPGs is the interaction between players unrestricted by traditional barriers of geography, age, gender, and race."

SALUDA TRAIL MIDDLE SCHOOL, COMPUTER GAMING CLUB

Student's Name: ____

Grade: ____

The computer gaming club at STMS will meet every Monday morning in the Media Center at 8:00 a.m. Students will participate for first semester only.

Student

As a student, I understand

- I will only be allowed to play the games my parent checked below.
- I will not share my username.
- The first time I am caught on a site not listed below, I will receive a warning. The second time, I will be removed from the club.

Signature: ______________________________________ Date: __________

Parent

Below is a list of games we will be playing in the Computer Gaming Club. Please check below the games your child is allowed to play.

_____ Runescape, www.runescape.com

_____ Age of War, www.maxgames.com/play/age-of-war.html

_____ Dragon Fable, www.dragonfable.com

_____ MechQuest, www.mechquest.com

_____ Adventure Quest, www.battleon.com

_____ BrainPOP, www.brainpop.com

_____ Poptropica, www.poptropica.com

Signature: ______________________________________ Date: __________

If you have any questions about the computer gaming club, please feel free to contact one of us.

Liz Martin, Media Specialist

Amanda Cavin, Media Assistant

As with gaming clubs, there are other youth groups that are increasingly taking advantage of the power of social networking venues for motivating and supporting young people outside of school. These outside-school activities serve some students who are not served at school. As Frank Baker notes, "There is no doubt that putting media tools in the hands of young people empowers them. They want to be heard, and they want their productions to be seen."

It's fitting that some of these empowerment tools are being put to use in unofficial contexts, after school, for youth who may often be disenfranchised by traditional schools. Mollie Blackburn, assistant professor at Ohio State University, has volunteered since 2002 at Kaleidoscope Youth Center, a local center for lesbian, gay, bisexual, transgender, and questioning (LGBTQ) youth in Columbus, Ohio. She describes her main research focus as studying "ways that LGBTQ youth and their allies engage with LGBTQ-themed novels in an out-of-school queer-friendly context." Mollie describes the work of the center as "an on-going balancing act, of allowing youth to explore resources and connect with other LGBTQ people and of ensuring their safety." This tension recently came to the surface when the center had to decide whether to have a page on MySpace and/or Facebook. While the youth at the Center felt this would open it up to a broader base of teens, many adults involved were concerned about lack of control over the message. The adults, however, listened to the teens, and the center is currently trying out social networking sites as a way of reaching out to LGBTQ youth.

The center is just in the early phases of using social networking sites, but Mollie describes how these sites quickly became essential. She describes the computers as being always in use, with students online, sometimes talking about what they are encountering, sometimes just working by themselves. As mentioned, the center was very sensitive to the security issues surrounding social networking and teens. As Mollie reports, this is something adults in the center are constantly working on, moving the computers to an open, visible space and limiting youth privacy online, for example. "We have also developed policies that prohibit anyone from accessing pornography in the center and from meeting up with someone they have met online while at the center," she says. "The consequence for breaking these rules is to lose access to the computers."

Whatever the reasons are, there are some uses of social media that aren't presently sanctioned for in-school uses, although it is clear that many of these uses of social media tools are still "educational" in nature. Through examining these models of instructional delivery that exist outside of the school day, we may find a way to better integrate them into the school day.

QUESTIONS TO CONSIDER

1. Can participating in games be a legitimate activity in schools? Are games just for entertainment value?
2. Can you think of a time when you learned something either about yourself or about the world by playing a game?
3. Is talking before, during, and after the playing of a game "on-task" behavior or "off-task" behavior?
4. Are there some issues that should always be consigned to "afterschool" time? If so, why, and who should decide?

This chapter has presented portraits of educators who are doing their work in extremely unfiltered classroom situations, including some projects that exist outside of the school day. Chapter 6 provides some overarching questions that remain after having looked at "Short," "Tall," "Grande," and "Venti" educational samplings.

A Blog Post From the Field

Over the last few weeks, we've ended up involved in some interesting discussions in class. We like to talk in our classroom. Sometime a lot. Our topics range far and wide but sometimes end up back at issues of technology, safety, and online habits. One thing that interested me lately was the fact that of the kids in my class who use social networking sites (which is almost all of my class of 24), the only one they want to talk about is Facebook.

Asking about television, three of my students claimed they watched, on average, three-plus hours of TV each day, but most of them said they watched less than an hour. Asking what they did instead, their answer as a class was not surprising: go online. I feel sorry for television marketers who have to deal with this generation. They all said that they might have several shows they watch in a week, but if they are just looking for something to do, they are more likely to head to their computers than their TVs. Boys are heavier gamers than girls, but even among them, games such as World of Warcraft, which involves a lot of teamwork, coordination, and a heavy social component, were the favorite. Is this their social network?

Overall, these have been interesting discussions. It has reaffirmed a lot of what . . . I've been thinking about lately. Kids expect to interact with their media. While they have not abandoned television completely, they are savvy prosumers who want to take part.

Clarence Fisher
Eighth-Grade Teacher
Joseph H. Kerr School
Snow Lake, Manitoba, Canada

6

"*Refill*"

Continuing the Dialogue

This book has been organized by questions, and so is this final chapter, which returns to some of the overarching themes we educators continue to encounter as we grapple with the implications of screen-based communication tools.

Will Social Networking Be Used to Free Students or More Tightly Limit Their Freedoms?

When I was a high school teacher, I often thought the transition in the monitoring of students was abrupt as they graduate from high school. I usually had to cover a study hall as part of my schedule, and I remember thinking how odd it was that we, as a society, expect 17-year-olds, 18-year-olds, and some students up to 21-year-olds to ask permission to leave a study hall, while the very next day, after graduation, their whereabouts are their own business. This kind of in-school restriction seemed arbitrary and unnecessary to me when I was in the midst of it. What was the reason that every 17-year-old student had to be accounted for at every moment of the school day, even to the point of monitoring his or her bathroom habits?

The reasoning behind such monitoring, of course, comes back to the custodial function that schools have served for many years, with schools serving "in loco parentis." Not only do we have to protect them from the mean world, but also we have to protect them from themselves. We certainly don't want them to be "smoking in the boys' room"! But are these kind of custodial functions of education overdue for a major reconsideration? Could Liz Boeser's hybrid class (profiled in Chapter 5), for example, become a model for how kids could do some of their work at home, or at least not always in school? In addition, could some of the activities that now have to be removed to afterschool activities be moved into the school day (whatever that school day may end up looking like)?

Paradoxically enough, kids who are free of adult supervision seem to fascinate us at the movies and in the stories we read. From the *Our Gang* comedies to *Catcher in the Rye*, from the *Home Alone* films to the Harry Potter saga, we are drawn to stories about literal or essential orphans; we want to explore the tension that exists when children are on their own, fending for themselves without adults fussing over them. This interest is not new. In the 1880s, Robert Louis Stevenson became transfixed with the real story that he read in the newspapers of a 16-year-old boy who was kidnapped by pirates and was able to get free, return to England, and prosecute his kidnappers; he based *Kidnapped*, in part, on this story. Charles Dickens could not let go of the orphan theme and wrote several novels not only based on his own difficult childhood but also on the challenged existence of so many children he observed in London. These examples of the orphan in fiction from over a century ago continue to find resonance today in film adaptations and even in modernized versions of them such as the Oscar-winning *Slumdog Millionaire*.

But that's all fiction. In real life, we don't want kids to be home alone. It is rare to find districts such as Liz Boeser's that allow students to do some of their work off campus. We just don't seem to be ready as a society to re-examine and perhaps re-conceptualize exactly what "childhood" should be, even as new media blur those lines for us between "childhood" and "adulthood" and "school" and "afterschool." And this kind of disconnect may be seen not only in relation to rules about such basic custodial issues as hall monitoring and truancy but also in our decades-long obsession with standardized testing. It's often unacknowledged that our insistence that everything that happens in a classroom be tied to a "grade" comes from these root feelings about childhood and what it's supposed to be like. One could argue that many of the conventions of childhood (Santa Claus, toys, sports teams) actually are constructions more for the pleasure of adults than for the pleasure of the children (see Joyce & Watkins, 2008, for dramatic pictorial evidence of this regarding Santa).

What, then, should be our responsibilities to young people in these new times? Is "childhood" a time that requires close monitoring and calibration? Or is it a time, especially as children enter secondary school, that begs for some freedom from those kinds of restrictions? Or do our responsibilities as adults lie somewhere in between as we attempt to structure environments that are, of course, physically safe while still allowing for some loosening of the collar?

A surprise in looking at the interview data for this book is how divided teachers are about these issues. Some seem rather unconcerned with how they will "grade" these social networking assignments. When I would ask my shopworn question, "Do you have a rubric?" I would often be met with silence from these teachers or a statement to the effect that rubrics are limiting. What indeed will happen to "assessment" and "grading" when the "product" that will be "graded" cannot even be visualized?

But on the other hand, there were a group of teachers interviewed for this book that seemed to take these new media and see opportunities for a heightened, very personal form of assessment, with teachers being able to see and have access to all of the students' work choices throughout an assignment. In a 21st-century classroom (and world), we clearly have the capability to monitor students 24 hours a day, even as some of us (and them) are voluntarily signing up to monitor ourselves in a very public way, sometimes on a moment-to-moment basis (see Twitter and Facebook). Students may not have to be physically at school (as in Liz Boeser's hybrid class), but they could actually be monitored just as closely as if they were physically there by way of an RSS feed going to the teacher each time something is modified, to name one example. One of Liz's colleagues suggested that students in the hybrid courses might have their computers monitored to prove when they were logging in. It could be just a step away that not only could their logging in be monitored but also where they go online as well. Cory Doctorow, in his book *Little Brother* (2008), has imagined a present-future of extreme student surveillance and what the implications are for those kinds of societal choices.

But no matter what side of the assessment issue they are on, the ethical dilemmas of using new media in the classroom are many and are also related to the custodial function of schools. The hard choices that must be made come up in almost every conversation I have with educators when they talk about social networking in schools. There are some teachers who at the very least seemed oblivious to organizational barriers that might deter them from incorporating social networking into their classrooms. They call the ways they circumvent these barriers "work-arounds." One technology evangelist I interviewed even suggested to teachers that they purchase wireless connect cards that bypass the school's network and allow the possessor to connect with the Internet no matter where they are. Other teachers go to extensive effort to get around filters and other blocks set up by their school districts. For example, if a school district blocks YouTube, the teacher might download the videos needed at home and take a DVD of those videos to school to show.

There are other teachers who go beyond the level of "work arounds." One teacher I interviewed was deep into introducing Ning to his sixth-grade classroom and taking them through the login procedures when he realized that Ning has a rule that kids under 13 are not permitted to use Ning. In a moment of indecision, he told the kids just to leave the default, showing that they were born on July 1, 1975. He rationalized this to the students by saying that it was like he was accompanying them on a field trip to a PG-13 movie. He had great educational experiences working on the Ning with his students for several weeks until a parent complained about something she had seen on her daughter's page. The teacher decided to stop using Ning with his sixth graders and feels that the platform he has gone to does not allow for the social interaction benefits that he got from Ning.

I am not advocating that teachers do what he did (nor is the teacher himself). The story is told only as an exemplar of the kinds of choices teachers are being forced to make regarding social media. These new screen-based literacies, to which our students are so attracted and at which many of them are so adept, add a new twist to the age-old debate regarding what degree of freedom children should be granted (and how we will define "children"). What does "in loco parentis" look like in this new arena of social networking?

What Is the Relationship Between Entertainment and Education?

Teachers also seem to be guilt ridden over what might be called "The Entertainment Factor" of these new media, worrying that, by opening up their classrooms to Web 2.0 and other new literacies, they disrupt the seriousness of school and "dumb it down." All this cyberspace activity is seen as too much fun for the kids with not enough "rigor."

Tom Liam Lynch is one of the last teachers I interviewed for this book. He serves as Technology Coordinator at New York City Lab School, continuing to teach during the day while helping other teachers integrate technology into their classrooms. "I became intrigued with what it means to use other media in the English classrooms," he says. One of Tom's first projects was to audio record responses to student papers. In his second year, instead of writing poems in response to *Passage to India*, the students audio recorded them, and Tom posted them online. "Kids started coming in with poems on their iPods that their friends had written," Tom recalls. He and his students started looking at the ways rap artists use assonance and alliteration. The students were posting classroom materials on their MySpace pages and listening to each other's creations on their iPods. There was quite a lot of connecting between groups as a result of this assignment, Tom felt.

But there were storm clouds on the horizon. Tom felt the students were losing the literary critique element of the project: "When they 'transposed' from their academic essays into their raps, they lost the argument that was essential." The next year, he created a *Romeo and Juliet* project in which they first did a straight literary criticism paper. Students picked up on issues in the text such as teenage sexuality, drug use, violence, and familial discord. Since he teaches in New York, Tom required them to write a kind of Regents-exam essay (the Regents being the famous statewide New York test for high school students) regarding these themes based on what they had done in class. "The next challenge for students after they got through that Regents gate was to work in groups, as they composed a rap, with each group centered around a theme represented in the text, attempting to keep some kind of literary criticism argument intact. That last part was really hard for them." Tom felt again that, when they recorded their raps, most of the groups lost the argument thread, becoming less focused on that goal of the assignment than on the rap elements (beat and rhyme, for example) in the texts they produced. Students were excited about the raps they produced and were sharing them in social networking venues; they were deeply engaged with the assignment. They were listening to their projects on their iPods as they rode the subway to school. But Tom continued to have doubts about what exactly it was that this project was teaching them.

> I felt like a failure. In early drafts of essays, they were making a good argument. When they got into their groups, they were composing to a beat, and they would get so interested in the rhyme—the rap genre was so powerful and embedded. I was trying to create that third space (Lynch, 2008), bringing in the pop culture with the academic. For the students at the end of the day, their pop space was much more powerful. In the end, these texts have lives way beyond the classroom. I think that won out in the end. It was more important for students to have something they enjoyed listening to than to fulfill my academic responsibilities.

This kind of deeply conflicted story comes up again and again, both from teachers who "buy in" to using Web 2.0 and new literacies in their classrooms and from those who don't. Teachers worry that students who are composing raps and posting them on their MySpace pages, for example, are getting caught up in the fun of the media and losing sight of whatever academic content is also involved. There is a very solid binary that comes through very strongly from educators between "education" and "entertainment." But a question worth exploring may be, "Does there really have to be that great divide?" As Lynch describes, he felt he was losing some of the "education" element in that his students were getting away from the Regents kind of literary criticism essay. But were the "arguments" expressed by his students any less worthwhile or "literary" because they were expressed in rap form rather than in a five-paragraph essay? Was there a power and inherent argument making just in the driving beat itself, not to mention the drive to share that beat in a social networking site? Perhaps we as educators need to be thinking about different forms of expression and respect the power of these new forms rather than regarding them as "mere" entertainment. After all, Shakespeare's plays were written and enjoyed as popular entertainment!

Is There Enough Time in My Schedule for Social Networking?

Often, a hesitation expressed by teachers about using Web 2.0 revolves around whether they have time to "fit" new media into their already crowded curriculum. "Will I have to take time to teach them how to work with a Ning?" is a commonly heard question. "I barely have time to get through my curriculum map as it is without throwing in a five-day tutorial on using iMovie." Teachers tend to feel that they need to get students completely comfortable with whatever tool they're using before making an assignment. And they feel they have to do it themselves. Actually, this is one of the easier questions in this chapter to provide some answers for.

After having interviewed many teachers who do integrate new media and new social networking opportunities into their classrooms, I have found that they have dealt with the time issue in two overarching ways. One way is to take minimal class time on demonstrating technology skills and to rely on students to give brief tutorials to each other either during class time or after school. In my own classroom, I've given up the constant struggle to remain on top of the latest technology development and to be able to demonstrate it for a large group. For one thing, the technology changes so rapidly that it's hard to remain an "expert" for long. And I've also noticed that teaching these kinds of technology skills in a large computer lab is a waste of time, in that students just want to get online and try them immediately (or check their e-mail or MySpace page). They don't want to listen to the teacher lecture on how to set up a blog. It's almost impossible to resist the lure of that keyboard ready for you to try what is being demonstrated.

Rather than follow this computer lab model, I'm increasingly relying on some of my tech-savvy students to teach minilessons that briefly introduce the technology or application being used using a projector in my own classroom or in small groups. Sometimes I even tap a student who is not tech-savvy to do the tutorial because sometimes they are the best guides to the steps that beginners must follow when mastering a new task. I've also found that many of the social networking tools have become so user-friendly that almost no technical explanation is necessary. Blogger.com, for example, shows the viewer how to set up a blog in three easy steps. It is not as complicated to teach these new media skills as it was back in the old days of the 1990s when technology teachers were making students learn DOS before being allowed to surf the Internet!

Another trend for coping with the time issue is to build choice into assignments. Teachers who may be concerned that they don't have time to thoroughly explicate how to navigate a Ning or use iMovie might consider not putting pressure on themselves and the students and simply make those optional choices in a long list of possible texts that students may compose. I make sure that students are not trapped trying to express themselves using some medium with which they're not comfortable (or I group uncomfortable students with more comfortable students to lessen the shock). Even though not all students today are "digital natives," most teachers will be hard pressed these days to have a class that doesn't have at least a few kids who are extremely proficient with technology, and those students will embrace the choices made available to them.

Of course, one question that is not so easy relates to these more reluctant students. Is it wise to challenge them to attempt to create in these new text forms? If we don't teach these skills at school, if we say we don't have the time, when will these skills be learned? If it's not true that all students are "digital natives," we need to make sure that, yes, all students are exposed to a breadth of curriculum content, but that they are also able to "read" and "write" about this content in all the forms that are now available to them.

What Should Our Schools Aspire To?

When asked why he continues to teach using blogs, Ken Rochester answered, "Because I did not benefit from traditional high school teaching; I cannot teach that way." The teachers in this book persevere, following an idealized picture they have of school that others in their buildings may not share. Many of them say that the benefits of persevering are mostly their own. William Chamberlain writes, "The biggest positive change has been with my own excitement over using the new tools and the experiences I am sharing with my students. I love finding tools that they can use that are different from my personal experience. I love sharing with other educators what my class is doing. I have more enthusiasm for teaching and for learning."

Zac Chase writes, "We've been looking for the silver bullet all the time. There's not a tool that will get my kids to learn. The tools just give permission for the teachers to be creative, and creativity is the key."

The teachers described in this book believe passionately in what they do, in imagining a better school for themselves and the students they teach. But what about the rest of us? Do we really want to change? Do we really want to imagine what this change could look like? Or are we comfortable with the status quo? As I visit schools across the country, I still see the same practices enacted with almost ritual fervor no matter what the setting and despite the fact that a majority of the people enacting these rituals are tired of them. Or are they? When are we going to start "walking the walk"?

Of course, this begs the question of whether it's possible to bring these new ideas into schools as they are now configured. Will they lose something in the translation? Five years ago, I asked if these new media would simply become the "spoonful of sugar to make the medicine go down." I wrote, "What will happen to new literacies in schools? Will something 'authentic' become 'nonauthentic' once it gets [there]?" (Kist, 2005, p. 140). Are the ideas documented in this book diluting and even corrupting the original intent of the social media involved? Or are they opening up new ways of "doing school" and helping to lead the way to a complete reconceptualization of teaching and learning in a mass society?

One of the educators interviewed for this book told me that the biggest obstacle to real reform in her building are the filing cabinets in the classrooms filled with old lesson plans and ideas. She said that so often teachers are just so tired that, after a few days of trying something new, they will burn out and eventually fall back on the filing cabinet—"the way they did it last year"—just to make things easier for a few weeks until they gain some steam and are ready to break the pattern again. She said, "If only I could get rid of those filing cabinets."

I think that too as I walk around the schools that I visit. Where would we be if we could get rid not only of the filing cabinets but also a lot of the other stuff that has accumulated? What if we could start from scratch? Will the new media and Web 2.0 initiate that task for us and sweep us into an entirely new way of "doing" school? Or will these new tools simply be pushed and pulled so that they fit into the old mold?

What will our schools look like one hundred years from now? If they are substantially different, I believe it will be because of the pioneering visions of the teachers described in this book, teachers I met through my own personal learning network, teachers who represent all the many more out there who are like them.

Appendix

Sample Letters to Parents

NOTIFICATION ABOUT A CLASS BLOG

8–14–08

Parents:

I am really excited about the possibilities we have available in class this year. Last year, my homeroom class created personal blogs that we used in class. This year, all fifth-grade students will have a blog to use in class.

I will monitor all blog posts to make sure that the students keep the entries both safe and appropriate. Comments to the blog will also be moderated to keep them safe and appropriate. I do not allow the students or commentors to post personal information. I do not allow students or commentors to post personal attacks on other students.

I believe that the class blog allows parents more access to what happens in my classroom than is otherwise possible. The blog is accessible to everyone: parents, students, extended family, and people around the world. Several of my students have had comments posted on their blog entries by people from countries as far away as Australia. This gives the students a genuine audience that encourages them to spend more time and effort creating worthwhile, meaningful posts.

If you would like to check out the blog the URL is *noeltigers.com.*

You may also find the blog by typing *class blog* in Google. It will be on the first page of results under *Mr. C's Class Blog.*

If you would like more information about how we use technology in the class, please contact me.

Wm. Chamberlain

Home Phone:

School Phone:

E-mail: wmchamberlain@gmail.com

PERMISSION TO PUBLISH STUDENT WORK ONLINE

Dear Parent or Guardian,

This is a permission slip allowing student work to be published. By checking yes, you are agreeing to allow me to publish student work in a variety of formats this year.

One way I like to engage my students in classroom projects is to publish their work online. When students know their work is going to be published, they take it more seriously. It also gives parents the opportunity to see what their child is working on.

Here are a few of the projects we plan to work on this year:

- Publish at least one book on lulu.com.
- Write on a classroom wiki I created once every two weeks about independent reading. The Web page, Reading Log Wiki, is linked from my Web page, mrmayo.org.
- Post writing assignments online using a secure digital portfolio Weblog I've created for each student. The sites will be password protected, and students will be required to use only their first names.

Students will be required to follow a strict set of rules and guidelines or risk losing their Weblogs. To see examples of some of these projects from my previous classes, please visit mrmayo.org. If you have any questions or comments, do not hesitate to contact me.

__________ Yes, I give you my permission

__________ No, I do not give permission

Parent Signature: ____

Student's Name: ____

NOTIFICATION OF A HYBRID CLASSROOM OR ONLINE COURSE

Dear Parents, Guardians, and Families,

I will have the pleasure of working with your students for two consecutive terms in College Writing. This elective is designed for college-bound seniors. This class is designed as a hybrid course where students will work through face-to-face instruction and in an online environment. This means that students are not required to be in the classroom every day. *Please refer to the attached form from page three of your Registration Guide.* Students will be expected to meet as a large group for lecture, instruction, review, and test days. Students will also work in assigned writing groups that will meet face-to-face only on assigned days throughout the term. Please see the attached tentative schedule. Students must be present for large-group days and assigned-writing-group days. *Failure to attend on these days will negatively impact the participation part of the grade.* Missed days will result in the loss of credit. If a student's grade drops below 70%, that student may be required to attend every day until the grade improves. In addition, students may also opt to come into the classroom to use equipment and/or ask for extra help on days when they are not scheduled.

Students in College Writing will read and write about several novels as well as nonfiction selections. In the first term we will work in large groups, small groups, and individually on *The Perks of Being a Wallflower* and a book in the creative commons, *Little Brother*, which students may buy, borrow, or download from the Internet in a variety of forms. In addition, students will participate in an online role-play that will be monitored and assessed by University of Minnesota researchers. During the second term, we will analyze novels that may include *The Kite Runner, The Chosen, Speak, Montana 1948,* and *Beloved*. Students will also work on an individual book project using novels selected from lists recommended for college reading. Students will review vocabulary, literary terms, and writing techniques in order to prepare for standardized tests and a wide variety of academic papers. Students will review and implement research skills in order to evaluate the merit of sources, consider forms, write for specific purposes and audiences, and use MLA format. You may also want to purchase *Write for College: A Student Handbook* (2007) hardcover (ISBN 978–0-669–00044–3) and softcover (ISBN 978–0-669–00031–3) for yourselves from a bookstore or online. Just make sure is it the same book we have in class.

During scheduled class time, computers and the Internet will be available, but it would be a benefit for each student to have Internet access away from school as well. Students will need the Internet in order to research their assignments, access the class Web site, communicate outside of class, and hand in assignments to www.turnitin.com. Each student must create a Gmail account in order to access the tools we will use in this class. Students will need to read and respond to each other's work in these formats. These blogs and wikis (and any other Internet sources) through which we publish our work must only be used for College Writing and therefore must be appropriate for school. *Any crude, illegal, or dangerous behavior included or alluded to in the assignments may be reported to a school counselor, administrator, and/or civic authorities.* Students will be able to access instructions, assignments, and work through this URL: http://missboeser.googlepages.com.

Please sign the form on the reverse side of this letter, detach it, and send it back with your student. Your signature on this form counts as an assignment in the course. Please feel free to contact me you have any questions. I am very eager to

(Continued)

(Continued)

start a new term and meet my new students. Thank you for your time and attention to your student's education.

Sincerely,

Elizabeth A. Boeser

Communication Arts and Literature

Thomas Jefferson High School

4001 West 102nd Street

Bloomington, MN 55437

E-mail: eboeser@bloomington.k12.mn.us

A student's grade will be divided into the following components:

- 45% ACADEMIC WRITING: Essays must be handed in on paper with a Turnitin originality report.
- 30% PARTICIPATION:
  - BLOG, WIKI, and NING: Each student is required to post journal entries online.
  - CLASS DISCUSSION and WRITING GROUPS: Students will respond in class to literature, nonfiction, and journal posts, as well as work together to proof and edit papers.
  - PEER REVIEW: Students will read and respond to the work of their peers in writing groups.

- 10% HOMEWORK, including vocabulary assignments and daily assignments.
- 5% TESTS AND QUIZZES on novels and nonfiction from class, including vocabulary.
- 10% FINAL EXAM on novels, stories, or terms we have covered in class.

NOTE: Late work will be given no more than half credit. No exceptions. No excuses.

All of the school rules apply in College Writing. Please *make sure you and your student know the school rules*. I will not tolerate any inappropriate or unacceptable behavior.

Please detach along this line and return the bottom portion with your signature.

Student Name: ____

I have read and understood Miss Boeser's letter and the course grading criteria. If we have any questions, we know we can contact Miss Boeser at her e-mail address listed above. I can be reached with any concerns, questions, or information regarding my student at (please circle preferred method):

(Phone) ____________________ or (e-mail) ____________________

Parent Signature: ____

Student Signature: ____

Hybrid Courses

Due to the nature of an advancing technological society and the need for our students to have 21st-century skills, Jefferson is offering a new type of course starting in the 2008–2009 school year. Hybrid courses combine the best components of face-to-face instruction with the flexibility of meaningful online instruction.

What makes a course a hybrid course?

Students will meet some days in class but will not come to class every day. For example, a hybrid course might meet on Monday, Wednesday, and Friday but not on Tuesday and Thursday. Some course content such as journaling, presentations, and research will be delivered online, and some work may be turned in online as well.

Are hybrid courses easier or harder than other courses?

Hybrid courses are not easier or harder but offer the same strong curriculum delivered in a different way. A student taking a hybrid course will be spending at least the same amount of time completing assignments as a student would in a traditional course.

Why should I take a hybrid course?

Hybrid courses offer a flexibility that can fit well with some learning styles. To succeed in such an environment, you need to be an independent learner, well organized, disciplined, and on-task. Students who have motivation, good time management, and technology skills will likely do well in a hybrid course.

Should I take a hybrid course?

Freshmen are not allowed to take hybrid courses. Answer the following eight questions to see if you are a good match with hybrid courses.

I have good time management skills and can stick to a schedule without prodding and reminders from a teacher.

Yes No

(Continued)

(Continued)

I am resourceful at figuring out what to do next when I hit a roadblock in following instructions.

Yes No

I am *not* a procrastinator.

Yes No

I would rate my reading ability at "Above Average" or higher.

Yes No

I express myself fairly well in writing.

Yes No

I would rate my technology skill level at "Above Average" or higher.

Yes No

I have access to a computer and the Internet at home.

Yes No

I am good at problem solving technical difficulties on the computer.

Yes No

6–8 Yes answers—you are a good candidate to take hybrid courses.

4–5 Yes answers—you may struggle if you choose to take hybrid courses.

0–3 Yes answers—you should avoid taking hybrid courses.

References

Atwell, N. (1998). *In the middle: New understandings about writing, reading, and learning* (2nd ed.) Portsmouth, NH: Heinemann.

Barton, D., & Hamilton, M. (1998). *Local literacies: Reading and writing in one community.* London: Routledge.

Borsheim, C. (2004). Email partnerships: Conversations that changed the way my students read. *English Journal, 93*(5), 60–65.

Brown, D. (1999). Promoting reflective thinking: Preservice teachers' literacy autobiographies as a common text. *Journal of Adolescent & Adult Literacy, 42*, 402–410.

Brownlow, K. (1969/1976). *The parade's gone by*. Berkeley, CA: University of California Press.

Burke, J. (2000). *Reading reminders: Tools, tips, and techniques*. Portsmouth, NH: Heinemann.

ChildStats.gov. (2008). *American's children in brief: Key national indicators of well being, 2008.* Retrieved November 15, 2008, from http://www.childstats.gov/americaschildren/index.asp

Chudacoff, H. P. (2007). *Children at play: An American history*. New York: New York University Press.

Doctorow, C. (2008). *Little brother*. New York: Tor.

Eagleton, T. (1983). *Literary theory: An introduction*. Minneapolis: University of Minnesota Press.

Eggers, D. (2006). *What is the what: The autobiography of Valentino Achak Deng*. New York: Vintage.

Garmston, R. J., & Wellman, B. M. (1992). *How to make presentations that teach and transform.* Alexandria, VA: ASCD.

Gee, J. P. (2003). *What video games have to teach us about learning and literacy*. New York: Palgrave Macmillan.

Hobbs, R. (2010). *Conquering copyright confusion*. Thousand Oaks, CA: Corwin.

Joyce, D., & Watkins, N. (2008). *Scared of Santa: Scenes of terror in Toyland*. New York: Harper Paperbacks.

Kist, W. (2000). Beginning to create the new literacy classroom: What does the new literacy look like? *Journal of Adolescent and Adult Literacy, 43*, 710–718.

Kist, W. (2003). Student achievement in new literacies for the 21st century. *Middle School Journal, 35*(1), 6–13.

Kist, W. (2005). *New literacies in action: Teaching and learning in multiple media*. New York: Teachers College Press.

Koch, K. (1970). *Wishes, lies, and dreams: Teaching children to write poetry*. New York: HarperCollins.

Kress, G. (2003). *Literacy in the new media age*. London: Routledge.

Kubey, R., & Baker, F. (1999). Has media literacy found a curricular foothold? *Education Week*. Retrieved September 15, 2008, from http://www.frankwbaker.com/edweek.htm

Lahr, J. (1969/2000). *Notes on a cowardly lion: The biography of Bert Lahr*. Berkeley: University of California Press.

Loomans, D., & Kolberg, K. (1993). *The laughing classroom*. Tiburon, CA: H.J. Kramer.

Lynch, T. L. (2008). Rereadings and literacy: How students' second readings might open third spaces. *Journal of Adolescent & Adult Literacy, 52*(4), 334–341.

McBride, J. (1996). *The color of water*. New York: Riverhead Books.

McLaughlin, M., & Vogt, M. (1996). *Portfolios in teacher education*. Newark, DE: International Reading Association.

Mintz, S. (2004). *Huck's raft: A history of American childhood*. Cambridge, MA: The Belknap Press of Harvard University Press.

O'Brien, T. (1990). *The things they carried*. New York: Broadway.

Pew Internet and American Life Project. (2008). Retrieved June 22, 2009, from http://www.pewinternet.org/

Prensky, M. (2005). Listen to the natives. *Educational Leadership, 63*(4), 8–13.

Richardson, W. (2003). Web logs in the English classroom: More than just chat. *English Journal, 93*(1), 39–43.

Romano, T. (1995). *Writing with passion: Life stories, multiple genres*. Portsmouth, NH: Boynton/Cook.

Romano, T. (2000). *Blending genre, altering style: Writing multigenre papers*. Portsmouth, NH: Boynton/Cook.

Savage, J. (2007). *Teenage: The creation of youth culture*. New York: Viking.

Schofield, A., & Rogers, T. (2004). At play in fields of ideas. *Journal of Adolescent & Adult Literacy, 48*, 238–248.

Silberman, M. (1996). *Active learning: 101 strategies to teach any subject*. Boston: Allyn & Bacon.

Smith, K. (1999). *Mental hygiene: Classroom films 1945–1970*. New York: Blast Books.

Taba, H. (1967). *Teacher's handbook for elementary social studies*. Reading, MA: Addison-Wesley.

Wilhelm, J. D. (1997). *You gotta be the book: Teaching engaged and reflective reading with adolescents*. New York: Teachers College Press.

Index

The Corwin logo—a raven striding across an open book—represents the union of courage and learning. Corwin is committed to improving education for all learners by publishing books and other professional development resources for those serving the field of PreK–12 education. By providing practical, hands-on materials, Corwin continues to carry out the promise of its motto: **"Helping Educators Do Their Work Better."**